35 Things
Your Teen Won't
Tell You, So I Will

35 Things
Your Teen Won't
Tell You, So I Will

Ellen Pober Rittberg

To my mother, for taking me to the library a lot and reading to me and encouraging me in whatever I do and have become. She didn't feed me junk food and taught me to brush after meals.

To my children, who are terrific, despite everything contained herein. When they were babes, I promised myself I wouldn't write about them . . . but the temptation was too great to resist.

Turner Publishing Company
200 4th Avenue North • Suite 950
Nashville, Tennessee 37219
(615) 255-2665

www.turnerpublishing.com

35 Things Your Teen Won't Tell You, So I Will

Library of Congress Cataloging-in-Publication Data

Rittberg, Ellen Pober.
 35 things your teen won't tell you, so I will / Ellen Pober Rittberg.
   p. cm.
 ISBN 978-1-59652-554-2
1. Parent and teenager. 2. Teenagers. 3. Parenting. 4. Teenagers--Family relationships. 5. Adolescent psychology. I. Title. II. Title: Thirty-five things your teen won't tell you, so I will.
HQ799.15 .P
649'.125--dc22

                    2009038275

This is a book of humor. Please note that any information in this book is meant for discussion only. Nothing contained herein is intended or is purported to be legal, medical, educational, or psychological advice. Before taking any action related to your child's mental or physical health, you should seek the advice of a medical or healthcare professional.

Printed in China

10 11 12 13 14 15 16 17—0 9 8 7 6 5 4 3 2 1

What a piece of work is man,
How noble in reason,
How infinite in faculties,
In form and moving how express and admirable,
In action how like an angel,
In apprehension how like a god!

~William Shakespeare, *Hamlet,*
Act II, Scene 2

Contents

Introduction:
What this book will do

This book focuses on 35 simple things, or rules, that offer insight on understanding and raising your teens. It will warn you about some of the bad things your teens will do. (Hopefully, you are not far from your home with a cast of a thousand teens partying there.)

It may make you worry less, because although you now know oodles of things to worry about you may not have known before, you can write yourself "To Worry About" lists and then feel vaguely superior for about ten seconds about how organized you are. In other words, you will have become an educated worrier. Worrying comes with the parent-of-a-teen turf. It's part of the job description. If there were a monument to parents of teens, it would consist of one massive Mount Rushmore–sized collective furrowed gray brow. (Or possibly, our symbol should be a bucket of sweat? Particularly for women of a certain age.)

It will make you feel you are not alone and that there is

intelligent life out there somewhere. Just don't ask where for the next couple of years.

It tells you that you belong. Whatever kind of parent you are—old, young, energetic, lethargic, depressed—parents of teens are all in this soup together. Welcome. Even if you weren't a joiner, you now belong to a club with no dues, no mission statement, and no common purpose except to not allow your teen to drive you cuckoo.

It teaches the inner workings of a teen's brain, which is scary if you think about it any longer than it takes to read this sentence. (It also means this book may get classified in the library under Horror or Science Fiction.)

It teaches alternative techniques to tearing out one's hair or reading about the pharmacological properties of hemlock. One such technique, shedding real or fake tears, can sometimes induce a momentarily guilt-laden teen to do what a parent wants.

It reminds you that your teen is that same cute little creature with the bobbing head you lavished so much attention on, who could always be counted on to provide your shoulder with an endless stream of regurgitated milk before you left your house each morning. Only now the teen is regurgitating on his friend's shoulder. And the present-day upchuck is not from milk but from that all-important teenage food-pyramid group, Fermented Grain Products.

It tells you of the need to keep a picture of your teen with you at all times. (Personally, I've always had trouble picking my children out in a crowd, beginning with Day One in the hospital nursery. But maybe that's just me.) If nothing else, it will remind you what your girl really looks like, beneath all that makeup that most closely resembles people on cheesy public access television shows at three in the morning. The photo will also help identify your boy-teen when you pick him up at the airport from a vacation and discover he's become a bottle blond.

This book may give you just the right amount of 'tude (attitude) so that for five seconds, maybe your teen will think you're nobody's fool (except perhaps Shakespeare's Fool. A brief review of your high school English notes may remind you that in Shakespeare, the only people who really knew which side was up were the Fools).

It will teach you to revive your old mantra from your child's Terrible Twos days: the word "no."

It will help you keep on top of your teen (and no, by that I do not mean sitting on him or her).

It will help you set realistic goals and standards. For example, 8:00 P.M. is not a realistic bedtime. Tucking your teen into bed is a bit over the top. It may, however, be a good guerrilla tactic when checking for random members of the opposite sex in the bed. And it is not a reasonable goal to surf the Web to try to find a chastity belt. However, purchasing a residential high-voltage electrified perimeter fence might be worth the cash.

This book will also teach you of the need to develop a fierce look resembling that of a prehistoric tribal chieftain living 30,000 years ago. Find a large mirror with good lighting. Practice it. That and a fully upturned snarling lip are must-haves in your parent-of-teen arsenal.

Please Note

If I seem to use a lot of military images, I do. Raising teenagers is a lot like war without the gore.

How I came to write this book

When I was pregnant with my first child, I did what I thought was a responsible thing: I read loads of books. I did not come from a large, extended family. The only thing I recalled about babies was that I wanted to pinch my baby sister when I was a child.

To remedy my black-hole information gap, I took a free course at a local department store (or was it a local hospital?) where I learned such basics as how to bathe and burp a baby. The subsequent hollow, tribal-drumroll thump sound my hand made on my son's back did little to bolster my new-mommy confidence. Ditto my experience with baby-bathing. I have a dog-eared picture of my two-month-old son being given a bath in my kitchen sink—the sink technique being one of the many "useful" things the hospital course taught. He looks positively shell-shocked.

My technical shortcomings notwithstanding, I brought some strengths to the parenting table: I was enthusiastic. I had endurance from my training as a long-distance runner. And I had a sense of humor. (Perhaps that was the most important thing I possessed!) Fast-forward to the teen years: I found I could and would chase my teenagers down when they were flying out of the house with bogus excuses about where they were and weren't going. (A very necessary skill, I might add.)

As my children got older, I discovered the books that were out there about raising teenagers seemed too preachy or were written by psychologists or were too dense. (Or was it me? Whatever.) In any event, these books made me feel guilty that I wasn't more rigid or more grown-up or more whatever it was these books were asking me to be. So, I've written a book that is lighthearted and empathetic most of the time but which contains tips and pointers explaining the thoroughgoing orientation a parent of a teen needs. It is the book I would have liked to have.

Some Brief Background

I have three children. I had all three within three years and two months. Having three children close in age forced me to be practical if I ever wanted to get out of the house before the sun set each day. I developed rules and mental checklists. Diaper bag in car? Check. Diapers and bottles (and formula in the bottles) in the diaper bag? Check. Babies in the car? Babies in car seats? Key in the ignition? Adult non-toddler driver in the driver's seat? As the children grew, the items on the checklists changed and grew longer. Teens in the house? Teens' friends in the house? A parent or parents in the house? Liquor smell on teenager's breath? Glazed eyes on teenager? Et cetera.

Because I had my children so close, I had little time to reflect on anything. My only philosophies were ones that could be expressed in a sentence or less: Be suspicious. Use your common sense. Choose techniques that work. Smile, don't foam at the mouth.

I hope the reader will come to regard this book as a tool in the parent arsenal for days when the parent feels he is on a steep cliff, the canteen fell into the ravine, and there are no other ropes besides the tether (which the parent may very well be at the end of).

In the Interest of Full Disclosure

I have two distinct perspectives on teenager-dom: the personal and the professional.

The Personal

As stated previously, I had three close-in-age teens. This had one large benefit: I didn't have enough time to totally forget what I learned with each teen before the next teen was at the same stage of development doing similar (read that: stupid) things. Because I had teens of both genders, I can say with assurance that both genders do equally stupid things, some that are the same and some that are different. For example, male teens develop what seems to be a pathological urge to total any car they have not earned the money for, usually within two months of obtaining their drivers' licenses. Your female teens discover texting and then beg off any face-to-face communication with you, preferring to communicate only through closed doors or from a different floor and at opposite ends of the house.

The Professional

Up until two years ago, I represented children as an attorney in court for thirteen years. In my work, I frequently spoke to parents, school personnel, therapists, doctors, social workers, and, if there were drug and alcohol issues, drug and alcohol counselors. I have included some of the more useful information I have garnered from that experience. This setting also provided me the opportunity to see a wide range of parents and parenting, from truly awful to very, very good.

A Brief Word About Gender Issues

I should add that I have tried to raise my children in a gender-neutral fashion. Because of my lack of fashion sense or because it cost less to dress my daughter in her brothers' hand-me-downs, for much of her younger years, she wore her brothers' clothes, including cowboy shirts with the boys' names embroidered on them. (As she didn't have much hair for the first few years of her life, no one seemed to notice that she was male-clothing attired. But hey, the Victorians dressed their young boys in dresses. In some cultures men wear kilts.) The only person who seemed to object was my daughter's babysitter, who refused to toilet train my daughter until I provided her with something other than her brothers' Fruit of the Looms.

Being gender neutral, or trying to be, also meant that I produced three adolescents who could not sew (and who knew nothing about anything domestic except beer). Occasionally, all of them could be counted upon to vacuum, but usually only under duress. There is one noteworthy exception to my children's lack of domesticity: they all do laundry and have done so since they were preteens. (See my chapter devoted to this important and time-intensive subject, "Give your teenagers meaningful chores.")

To Know: Some Common Pitfalls

The following are some common excuses parents give when they miss the mark:

1) But my child promised . . . (Teenagers do not promise. They lie and twist the truth.)
2) I trusted my child. (Response: Why?)
3) But I thought my teenager was at . . . (Teenagers will say anything to get to the starting gate, i.e., the front door or the car.)
4) My brain is permanently warped from raising a teenager. (A good excuse. But take heart. The warping is temporary.)

You should resolve to improve as you go, and you will likely improve with each child (if you have more than one child). Of course, the oldest child will not appreciate that he is your learning curve. The eldest child will be quick to point out your shortcomings and insist quite stridently that you must shape up. My suggestion: let him be the parent (for ten seconds). The middle child, if you have more than two children, that is, will either always be slightly disgruntled or will always aim to please you. (Know, however, that he chooses what he is. Not you. Tough break.) The youngest child will accuse you of babying her or of not having taught all of the basic things she should know, or both. She will also accuse you of having large gaps in the photo album. All of which are true. But who can blame a parent? There's a lot of Attention Deficit Disorder out there, much of it belonging to parents of teens.

Full Disclosure: I Liked My Teens Most (Okay, Some) of the Time

Looking back, which is hard to do because my long-term memory is shot (or, more likely I have Post Traumatic Stress Disorder, having blotted out the truly horrible parts), overall, I enjoyed my teenagers (although they didn't always enjoy me!). It's possible that I enjoyed them as much as I did because a significant part of me is age eighteen mentally, emotionally, and physically (okay, delusionally) and holding.

Please Note

In this book, I give practical ideas and insights about parenting teenagers. However, nothing in this book is or should be construed as legal advice or opinion. Moreover, this book contains no guarantees. I share my information in the hope that insights of the battle-hardened have some use.

A Further Note

With rare exception, I have not identified any children or parents by name except that I will refer to my children as Big Boy, Middle One, and the Girl.

The 35 Things

~ Rule 1 ~

The family is not a democracy. It's anti-democratic and must be

Think of your family as a fiefdom in the Middle Ages. Your children are serfs without the work ethic. Parents are enlightened despots. A despot only knows one way to act: decisively. Despots don't waver. They rule with iron gauntlets. They must. Teens read passivity as weakness. And if they perceive you to be weak or gullible, they will step over, around, and on you. Do you want to be thought of as a waffler, a wuss, and a weakling? Do you really want treadmarks all over you, metaphorically speaking?

If you are not a natural leader, then you must instantly develop leadership abilities and the ability to think militarily. Think George Patton but don't slap your kids' faces. Think Winston Churchill but don't smoke cigars. Think cutting them off at the pass before they are at the pass. Think pincer movements and containment. Think Iron Curtain without the communism. Regard their bad behaviors as scourges and epidemics, to be wiped out, extirpated. And emphasize to your teens that there is only one Declaration of Independence and that it is in Independence Hall in Philadelphia.

To Know: Anarchy and Chaos Are Not Forms of Family Government to Which You Should Aspire

Teens are impatient people. They leap into things without thinking them through. They want what they want when they want it and usually yesterday. They don't like to hear "no" or variants thereof, such as "No way, José." If you are a somewhat undisciplined out-of-control sort (and even if you're not), pose the following question: Do I want my child to be just like me, or do I want a newer, more improved version? Read on if you have answered yes to the last part of the question.

To Do: Keep a Cool Head When Things Go South

When things go downhill, the natural tendency is for a parent's IQ to dip precipitously. This results in operating in crisis mode. Don't operate there, or try not to. Foresee problems before they come careening at you at ninety miles an hour. And if you are not a naturally suspicious person, become Alfred Hitchcock. See all the scary angles and dark places. Scrutinize your teens with eagle eyes. And ask yourself: Do my teens seem troubled, evasive, or worse, stoned? (And don't let them leave the house until you notice the whites of their eyes. And look them in the eye when they return from a night out. Have a staring contest, if need be.) Develop Mommy and Daddy Parent-of-Teenager Radar. If your teens are vague and evasive, pin them down like dead butterflies. Ask yourself: Does my teen seem different from yesterday or a month before? Has his personality (or the way he deals with me) changed in a short time? If so, chances are something is up, and up generally means bad when it comes to teens. Different also means bad most of the time. The only change that isn't bad is teens' normal-growth body-shape change, which may make you cringe but is not in your hands.

To Know

If your voice of authority includes a threat to do something or withhold something, you must do (or not do) whatever it was. However, rather than threatening, the better way is to tell the teen that if she acts a certain way, her action or non-compliance will have negative consequences. And learn to say the phrase "negative consequences" smoothly. Along with the word "no," "negative consequences" is your other mantra.

An example: The Big One was balking at the reasonable

curfew I had imposed. He told me that if I didn't raise his curfew, he would ignore it. I took a deep breath—deep breathing helps in such situations, I think. I then gave him the following speech, which you may adapt as you see fit for any direct challenge to your authority.

The Speech

> You will probably be living under my roof for the next few years. And it can be a very nice experience or a very unpleasant experience. As long as you live under my roof, you follow my rules.

Yes, that is an implied threat. And yes, you must mean it and say it with conviction and with a fixed eye. I suggest developing your own fixed eye. It should be part squint, part frown, and part wrath-of-the-ancient-unmerciful-gods. Practice it in the mirror. You will be using it.

To Do: Become an Approachable Authority Figure

Now that you are a leader, you must also convey to your teen that you won't do something rash that may bring you under the thumb of a real government (not your carefully constructed

Enlightened Despotic family government as described above). You want her to know you are a reasonable person and a good problem solver.

How do you do this?

Speak with the voice of authority even if you're not 100 percent certain that you're 100 percent certain. If need be, at a later date, you can alter your position, but not now, not when you've just taken a stand. Think Franklin Roosevelt (not Custer). Be decisive. If your child is too scared to come to you for advice (because your negative consequences are perceived by your teen to be too draconian), then he likely will spend a large proportion of his teenage years trying to avoid your detection. That will become his goal, and he won't know how truly wise you really are. He will also get into pickles that he won't be able to get out of.

I also suggest becoming aware of your body language when you speak to your teen. Avoid a lunge position. Try not to flail your arms like windmills. Parents of teens are supposed to be dignified even when their guts feel like Jello and they feel the irresistible impulse to rub their index finger up and down the lips.

~ Rule 2 ~

For every action, there must be a reaction

If there is one common characteristic of almost all teens, it is that they lie. Some of them tell whoppers. Some tell smaller lies. Others lie through their teeth. Still others are great liars. Whatever the case, when you catch your teens in lies having to do with their safety and well-being (such as throwing a party when you are out of town, underage drinking, or drug taking), the consequences must be severe enough and swift in order to have a deterrent effect. What punishments work best? Grounding for a month or more is good. Taking away the cell phone and iPod and computer privileges if the child has her own are other good ones. Driving privileges prohibited? That's good. Banning them from any form of transportation other than their own two feet? That's another good one. Do not deviate from the punishment you have chosen, with the exception of maybe a little bit of time off for good behavior if you think the lesson learned was really learned and only if your punishment was still adequate with the good time off.

A Word About Going to One's Room: A Definition

If your teen is grounded, grounded should mean a lack of pleasure. The confines of the grounding area must be spelled out, and the conditions. There should not be a television, computers, modems, cable or satellite hook-ups, video conferencing capability, iPods, piped-in music, lawnside serenaders, Game Boys, cell phones, other teenagers, siblings, a visit from Publisher's Clearing House, or any other means of stimulation. Think of grounding as prison solitary confinement, only with better food and toilet facilities.

To Know: Teens Have a Learning and an Un-learning Curve

If you think that once your teen has been punished, she won't ever lie to you or be sneaky again even though she's cried and apologized repeatedly, think again. It's not that she's not sorry, she really is at that moment. But the feeling sorry wears off like cheap perfume, or even good perfume after you wash. And when it does, she very well may do the same stupid or dangerous thing. Or some other stupid or dangerous thing.

To Know

There's no lack of stupid or dangerous things for your teens to think up to do that may screw up their lives, health, safety, and general welfare.

To Do: Emphasize the Need to Take Personal Responsibility

Part of becoming a responsible member of society is considering one's actions in advance before embarking on the act. If your teenagers can be eased into this thought-mode, their chances of becoming responsible people are greatly enhanced. Your job is to listen to their foolish explanations when they've done things you don't approve of. Walk them through their explanations, and explain to them why they're wrong. Avoid using adjectives like moronic and nouns such as twit, fool, and jerk. Try not to laugh like a hyena. Emphasize that some things are never right, like stealing, destroying other people's property, beating people up, being disrespectful to teachers, binge drinking, drug taking, and using foul language. If you use foul language when your emotions get away from you, develop alternative phrases like "fudge," "shoot," and "gee willikers."

To Do: Help Your Teen Develop Common Sense

Few people are born with common sense. Some never acquire it. Part of a parent's job is to not give teens any more responsibility than they can handle at a given time.

An example: When the Girl was a preteen, she groused bitterly to me that I was overprotective and that I had waited a ridiculously long time to allow her to go anywhere other than that part of the street where I could see her from my window. She asked me if when she got married would that be the first time she could walk somewhere without me. (I told her to ask me when we got to that day.) I reminded her of that day when she and her friend walked down the block and didn't stop. When I didn't see her from my window, I raced all over the neighborhood like a chicken without a head. Somehow I caught up with them, but not before I had aged 12 years. It hadn't dawned on the girls that they were supposed to stop or tell me where they were going.

This is a classic case of a lack of common sense, and specifically, a lack of sense about the cost of plastic surgery for the child's parents who age overnight prematurely. Teens have variable, shifting amounts of common sense, depending upon who they hang around. To the extent that you are able, choose how much your child will be exposed to and when that exposure will occur. (And don't ask that it be in a laboratory under sterile conditions, or ask that your children never be exposed to anything ever. Although that's a tempting goal.)

To Know: However Much Freedom You Are Thinking of Giving Your Teen, It's Probably Too Much

Allowing your high-school-aged teen to go on Spring Break vacation with her friends to a destination known to be a Spring Break college vacation town is either an act of misplaced faith or tomfoolery. Nevertheless, if you decide that with your (or her) hard-earned funds, your child should be permitted to be exposed to debauchery (or possibly doing the exposing) and a level of drinking and carousing that most roughly approximates ancient Rome during Nero or a bawdy house without any money changing hands, then by all means, buy the kid a nonrefundable ticket and say arrivederci.

To Ask Yourself: Am I Law Abiding?

Your attitudes shape your teen's view of the world. This sounds obvious but isn't to parents who think of themselves and their children as the privileged few. Allowing a child to drive a car anywhere other than to and from school and work when the child has a restricted work-study license gives the teen the message that rules don't apply to him. An out-of-control teen equals a future out-of-control adult. And out-of-control adults produce out-of-control teens.

To Know: If Your Teen Wants to Spend Extended Periods of Time with You, It's Abnormal. No Offense

It is common knowledge that teenagers consider their parents a necessary evil and an embarrassment. And, no, it's not your deodorant or your breath or the way you dress (although that may play into the mix). In your teen's mind, other teens are the only people worthy of your teen's consideration and lack of condescension. You start out your child's teen years feeling small. You progress through the teen years, feeling increasingly small and superfluous to the point of microscopic bugdom until:

1) Your child needs money;
2) Your child gets into trouble he can't figure his way out of (and even then, he will only come to you if he feels you are safe enough to come to); or
3) Your child needs a ride somewhere.

Teens' normal growth and development (and I use the term "normal" loosely) requires that they have friends and a peer group. So, even if it seems attractive at first blush, you should give up the idea of bankrolling your future financial happiness to become the first family to sign up for an extended trip to Mars. No matter what, your teen won't want to spend a lot of time with you even if you have great people skills and are a barrelful of monkeys. Which leads to my next principle: the most important influence on your teenager (by far) is not you or school, but your teen's friends.

– Rule 3 –

To know your children's friends is to know your children

Knowing your children's friends is no easy task. You barely know your teen. You are two ships passing, except his ship cuts a sharper image. Teens are notorious for giving the same stock answers they gave when they were in elementary school to questions such as, "How was school today?" (The most common answers: "Okay." "Good." "Bad." Or "Crunch, crunch," when they are eating.) Thus, it becomes harder to know what they're thinking and doing at any given moment.

To complicate matters, if you have a bad feeling about one of your children's friends and you don't know that child, you're not going to be able to formulate much of an argument as to why that friend is unsuitable. (And you may not always want to argue the point directly.) Your goal, then, is to get to know your teen's friends. The question is, how?

Establish eye contact. And notice that the whites of their eyes are clear and white, and the pupils non-dilated.

Engage in active listening. When your teens and their friends are at your house, keep your ears peeled. Which basically means you establish a listening post—your house, your car, anywhere where you can hear anything. Analyze the interactions. Are they whispering and being clandestine? Are they all charged up and ready to do . . . what? Engage your children's friends in what seems to be just friendly conversation. Disarm them. Flatter them. Be a guerrilla (as opposed to a gorilla. Although there are times for that too). Compliment them on some item of clothing or their hairstyle. They have blue hair? Tell them you love that shade of blue (and you're not lying. You do love that shade, only not on hair and not on your child's head specifically). And always listen carefully to their responses. If active listening does not yield the desired information, then do what is next best: eavesdrop.

To Do: Spy and Eavesdrop

Sometimes the only way you will find out what is really going on is by putting your ear to the wall or a cup to the wall (Dixie cups are good) or lingering on the stairs near a closed bedroom door, or any other means of hearing what is going on or being talked about right under your nose. You do this not because your life is dull (and dull and boring is good if it means

14

nothing unpleasant or unexpected is happening in your teen's life) but because you desperately want your teen to be safe. By eavesdropping, you sometimes may be able to figure out if something big and unpleasant will occur or has occurred.

An example: Teenager X seemed less energetic than normal, but his parent couldn't put his finger on it. The parent asked the teen if he was tired or if something was wrong. The teen said no. It was only after several friends visited the teen in rapid succession and they all retreated to his room and closed the door that the parent realized that something was up (and as stated previously, up is usually bad). The parent listened in and discovered that the teen had gotten jumped at a party by some teenagers from a rival school. The parent was then able to take the teen to the emergency room to check for internal bleeding, breaks, or sprains.

To Do: Carpool Whenever You Can

If you own a car, lease a car, or have access to a car, carpooling is a vital activity for you. It accomplishes a twofold purpose:

1) You get to know your children's friends in all their spontaneous exuberance.
2) You pick up valuable information.

The two points are interrelated. If your children's friends think of you as a fly on the wall, they will talk and will say things that may astound, perturb, and shock you. But these are things you need to know. Also, teens are big gossips. They love to talk about other teens, and you need to know what they are saying about these other teens, especially those involved in weird and extreme things. The more you know about your children's lives and friends, the better.

Of course, while listening, you will refrain from laughing, crying, letting your mouth drop open in disgust or amazement, or flaring your nostrils when hearing stories about neighborhood teens that sound too bizarre, extreme, and creepy to be true but most likely are.

– Rule 4 –

If you make your house a welcoming place, your teen's friends will come

It's better, much better, for teens to be in houses of responsible adults than hanging out outside local fast-food joints, on street corners, in deserted parks, or other even more remote locations where they are more likely to be out of reach of parental authority and thus are more likely to get into trouble. There is no lack of unsavory and negative influences on the streets such as street walkers, street vendors, vagrants, homeless people, deranged people, people in cars who might not see your teenager in the street or sitting on the curb with their feet sticking out, drunk drivers, kidnappers, and kids from rival schools looking to start a fight. And this is only a partial list. Moreover, if your kids spend any amount of time outdoors, they end up smelling like the great outdoors (or wet llamas).

What makes a house welcoming? Food. TV. A good stereo system. Video games. Friendly parents. Warmth, both heat-wise and parent-wise, that is.

~ Rule 5 ~

To supervise a teen party, you must be everywhere

If your teenager has asked you if he or she can have a party at your house, you should feel good about it. It means your teen thinks you are normal enough that you won't totally shame him to pieces in front of his peers. But it also requires work on your part. Supervising such a party is a mammoth responsibility.

At bare minimum, you must make certain there is no alcohol or anything illegal or immoral going on in or around your house. This means you must move around your house at frequent intervals with the grace and fluidity of the Tasmanian Devil. And once again, drawing upon military imagery: march (without looking like you're marching) through your house. Close in on offensive elements. Make precision concentric circles in and around your house. Leave no area of your home uninspected throughout the night. And continue to do it again and again.

To Do: Circulate!

In short, be omnipresent. This gives the message to the teen guests that you are godlike and thus worthy of respect. There should be no question that they are on your turf and it is now your Benevolent Despot rules they are operating under, like it or not. But you should also give the kids the sense that you're happy they're there. Which you are. If nothing else, you now have an opportunity to meet some of your children's peers whom you have wanted to scrutinize and assess.

Understand that your teen will probably not be happy with you if you follow the above guidelines. He would prefer that you disappear up to your room in your fleece bathrobe and dorky mules. If your teen starts to get obnoxious and persists in demanding that you banish yourself to a far corner of your household, tell him flat out: I won't disappear. It's not happening.

You don't necessarily have to be obvious about being ubiquitous. It's better to play the innocent. Use sly methods. If your laundry room is located in a central area, start doing laundry or do bogus-laundry. (This requires putting some laundry by the washing machine before the guests arrive.) Wash out a few dishes (if your kitchen is centrally located and there are kids in your kitchen). Float down to the basement. Consider yourself a human surveillance system with an eye far more acute than any high-tech video camera, and far more intelligent.

You must also let all the kids who come to your house know that once they come to your house, they must stay put inside your house. They can't loiter on your lawn and carouse out in the street. They can't make noise outside your house. This is to protect the teens from themselves and you from your neighbors' wrath. Another thing you must do is (before and during the party) check to see that your teenager or their peers have not put any beer in or around your house.

If you do not circulate during a party enough times (which means continuously), unacceptable things will happen.

An example: It was the tail end of the party, and I walked into what I thought was a now-deserted den where I noticed the lights seemed unusually dim. There, on the couch, I found one of the Girl's friends and a boy entwined in body language that can best be described as two Japanese choking vines. I was none too pleased. I said nothing. My look magically unglued them and their lips. The embarrassed, guilty look on her face indicated that if I hadn't entered when I had, something far more embarrassing and inappropriate would have occurred.

When the doorbell rings, greet your children's friends. Be friendly and welcoming. Don't you want your children's friends in your house where they can be safe? You're happy they're there, you really are (or convince yourself you are). If their parents have reared them nicely, you will usually find that your children's friends are nice and polite and are happy to talk to you, if you make them feel genuinely welcome. And even if they haven't been reared particularly well, perhaps they will rise to your heightened expectations.

Question: What do I serve at teen parties?

Answer: Obviously, you don't serve liquor to underage drinkers.

When you choose the food and beverage items, serve things that don't stain. If you serve soft drinks, serve Sprite and 7UP instead of colored sodas. Serve dry things like pretzels and spread around a lot of paper plates and napkins. If you really want to have fun, you can make something funny to eat. I once made little melted marshmallow men with toothpicks for the Girl's friends which, for some reason, endeared me to them for years. They just thought I was so adorable, or at least my gesture of hospitality was. (I didn't have to let them know that I was incapable of baking anything that was both ornate and edible, did I?)

If something spills, wipe it up and move on. Chances are, if you supervise the party adequately, no one and nothing will get broken (and remember before the guests arrive, wisely put away anything valuable or any other objects that can be easily knocked over).

– Rule 6 –

If you don't approve of your child's friend, approach the matter as an international diplomat would

Analyze the Problem

First you must ask yourself what is it exactly you don't like about this person. Is it the way the teen looks? Is it the way the teen relates to you? Is it based upon reliable information? Or is it just a feeling? Sometimes that's all you have to go on. That and your own wildly pumping adrenaline.

To Do: Use Your Gut Instinct

Every now and then there may be a kid who comes along whom other parents you respect don't have a great feeling about. This is definitely a person you need to know more about directly or from reliable information. And you can bet dollars to donuts that there will be at least one of these types of friends during your teen's teendom. And they require immediate action on your part. Sly action.

To Know: You Need a Good Communication System

To the extent you have a good communication system, you may be able to find out about a problem kid from other parents even before you've met the kid yourself. One parent hears something this kid said, or observed that kid, or talked with him directly. So what do you do if you find one of these teens has glommed onto your teen or vice versa? You monitor the situation. You try to find out if your teen is suddenly doing something new and negative (and, as stated previously, new and negative usually go together). And of course, you try to give this new friend a chance. You engage him or her in conversation to find out if other parents' perceptions are on the money. But sometimes this is not always possible. This teen may be under the parent radar and thus is inaccessible by choice or can't be reached because he's a teen and you're an adult. And you can't go sniffing this teen out as if you were a pig pursuing a truffle.

**Question: Do I tell my child I don't approve of her
                   friend if I don't approve of her friend?**

23

Answer: Try not to tell her. Not right away, anyway.

If right off the bat you tell your child you don't like that kid, she will automatically defend that kid and get defensive. If you attack the friend, your teen takes it personally. What you need to do is marshal information. If you overheard this kid talking about staying out late or going to clubs where there's drinking and your child is underage, you're starting to get some evidence that this kid is an unsavory influence, someone you'd like to banish to a far end of the globe. Or, it may also be that any number of your child's current friends were beginning to talk about engaging in that behavior, but this teen made it all come together for them.

What you then must do is tighten the screws. Keep closer tabs on your child than normal. Get a phone chain going. Sound the general alarm. Bugles are good.

If you're certain your instincts are right and you have enough information to back them up, tell your teen why you would like to make a dartboard with this new teen's photo on it. Next, walk him through the reasons why you don't like the kid, and tell him why this new friend is not friend material. You may want to have a soundproof room ready for times like these. Don't expect him to drop this friend, but if your child has some respect for you, he may think about your words. And if you are lucky, that friend may fall out of your child's orbit. But usually, that doesn't happen immediately. It's a pride thing. Your teen wants it to seem (to himself anyway) that he dropped the friend of his own volition.

– Rule 7 –

Know thy children's friends' parents

The second-most-important thing for information-starved parents of teens (and parents of teens are by definition information-starved because no teenager is going to tell her parents much of anything useful unless it is twisted out of her in socially unacceptable ways) is: know thy children's friends' parents as if your child's life depended on it. And it could.

To Do: Develop Some Conversation Openers

Once I get to know my children's friends, I find it fairly easy to call the parents up and introduce myself to them. Usually the gambit goes something like this:

"Hi, I'm Big Boy's mom, and I just wanted to introduce myself to you. I figured anyone who did such a good job raising Eric is someone I want to meet."

At this point, that parent is totally disarmed (and if you asked that parent to buy a 100-dollar raffle ticket from you, he gladly would). Understandably, he is flattered. I'm telling that parent I approve of and like his kid, and I am giving him credit for producing him. Who wouldn't be open to future friendship? Now, when I say "friendship" I am not saying that I have to socialize with these parents (which I have occasionally done). I am saying that it is critically important that we as parents talk. We should talk from time to time, but preferably even more often if the occasion calls for it—and the occasion is that our children are teenagers. Ideally, we parents should all live in one kibbutz-like house so we can share information and monitor our children twenty-four hours a day. Sometimes the communication you've established will pay off.

An example: Big Boy's best friend was kind, mature, had a job, took care of his single mother who was chronically ill, and watched after his younger sister. I adored him. His mother, M., was frequently homebound. We developed a relationship that was largely conducted over the phone but proved to be an important one.

One Friday night, M. called me. Her son had called her from a noisy party of mostly high school upperclassmen our sons were at. (Our kids were in the ninth or tenth grade at the time.) She said he sounded scared, and she asked if I could go over and see what was going on. I was there in a flash, and boy, oh boy, were our boys glad to see me. The party had begun to rapidly escalate out of control and they wanted no part of it, but they weren't really sure what to do. At the time,

I wondered: Would my son have called me if his friend hadn't called his mom? I can honestly say I'm not sure. But if M. and I weren't comfortable calling each other, who knows what might have happened.

In short, parents of teens need each other badly, mostly for our teenagers' sakes and also for our own sanity. Looking back on it, I should have known that the party Big Boy and his friend were at lacked adequate adult supervision. In fact, I didn't really know where my son was that night. Which was a mistake. Big one. Big.

To Know: Think of Other Parents as a Network That Is a Combination of Interpol, the CIA, the FBI, and Whatever Else Is Out There

Other parents can sometimes fill gaps in your information system. Occasionally, they are a source of emotional support. Sometimes they are a lifeline. Other parents also are a good way to catch your teenagers when they concoct small or large lies. If your child says he is going to X's house and that X's mother will be there all night, and you call X's mom and she either knows nothing about this or says yes, the boys are coming over but she is going out, you have caught your child in a bald-faced lie.

A Partial List of Information You Need to Know That Other Parents Can Help You Know

1) The parents who allow underage teenagers to consume alcohol in their houses;
2) Which parents abuse alcohol or use illegal substances whose houses your children might be invited to;
3) Parents who allow children to congregate in their houses when they are not home;
4) Where your children really are at any given moment. (I'm convinced that whoever wrote the song "Give Me a Home Where the Buffalos Roam" was really not talking about buffalo but teenagers. Teenagers are always on the move.)

To Know: Some Parents Are Not the Nicest People. Be Prepared. You Still Have to Get to Know Them on Some Level

Although it might be convenient to consider all parents of teens as fellow members of some fun-loving, kindhearted large club such as, say, the Mouseketeers, that is not, strictly speaking, so. Other parents may not share your values or your kindness and generosity of spirit, if that description fits you. But if your children socialize with their children, you need to get to know these parents on some level, howsoever awkward.

An example: Once, when Big Boy was in the ninth grade, I rang the doorbell of the girl's house where there was to be a gathering. The girl was part of a group of around eight boys and girls who constituted a crowd my son seemed to be a member of. I figured it was high time to introduce myself to the father, who was the sole custodian of the girl. (The mother lived in a far-off state.) The father answered the door. He was dressed in overalls, which threw me off a little since he was a driver of a limousine (and from good information, I knew he didn't own any tract of land larger than his 60-foot-by-100-foot lawn).

"Hi," I said in my friendliest voice. "I'm Big Boy's mom and I just wanted to introduce myself to you." There was a dead silence. The father did not smile back. "I also just wanted to make sure that some adult was going to be home while my son is here."

"Yes," I think he said. (Or "Yeah," he said, or maybe he just grunted.) He didn't ask me or my son to leave, to his credit. But he also didn't ask me in or say "Have a nice day," or give me a yellow smiley sticker.

"Well, it was nice meeting you," I said, which wasn't true because it was awkward as hell. But it was necessary.

That was the only time I can ever remember a parent being less-than-cordial to me. If the man was offended, why was he? I didn't know him from Adam, and I had to get to know him on some level, even if it was just to let him know that I wouldn't let my son stay there if he or some responsible adult wasn't there. (And I use the term "responsible adult" loosely here.) I did not enjoy being treated as if I was a leper with zilch social skills. Being a parent of a teenager means doing all kinds of uncomfortable hard things, including interacting with people you would normally never interact with, such as Mr. Greenjeans.

– Rule 8 –

Be interested in what your teen is interested in, even though you would otherwise have zilch interest in it

Part of developing a relationship with your teen involves knowing what excites your teen, acting interested, and, when appropriate, sharing the enthusiasm, if you can at all muster it. And if you can't muster it, you must learn to fake it well.

In some cases, you will have to enter zones that you have zip knowledge in.

An example: My ultimate acting challenge came when my daughter took up team sports in earnest, playing three sports a year. Overnight I needed to go from Sports Bimbo to Sports Fan. Of all her sports, lacrosse posed the largest challenge. From the look of it, it would seem that it should be sort of like tennis, only it was played on a field. But no. It was far less genteel. Sometimes the girls banged their sticks hard and hit each other in the head. I also had a hard time trying to keep track of whose goal was whose, or which direction the ball ought to bc going in. This led to my not-infrequent cheering for the wrong team, usually when the score was neck-in-neck. Dubious benefits to me included savoring my Dunkin' Donuts coffee in 20-degree temperature while feeling my epidermis flake off my face on windy days. (Coffee tastes especially good at such moments.) I also felt particularly self-sacrificing and saintlike, given that I was rapidly attaining borderline-frostbite-victim status. A dubious benefit to my daughter was that her friends felt sorry for her mother's inability to understand the game and cheer at appropriate intervals.

To Know

It's important to show faux enthusiasm even if you would otherwise have no interest or have a natural aversion for the things you find yourself doing with your teen.

If your teen wants to play her favorite rock group's CD for you, then feel good about this and listen well (while paying special attention to the lyrics). And it's a good idea if you don't like it, to pretend that you do—if you don't object to the content.

For some strange reason, your child will likely choose at least one hobby and pursuit that is entirely alien to you.

An example: My daughter went through a heavy-duty thrift

shop wardrobe phase, which I possibly stupidly encouraged in the belief that it might lead to a career in fashion. Not only did I drive her to these stores, I frequently accompanied her into the places. There, I watched my daughter troll the aisles of musty alpaca jackets and faux-Gucci-print pants while I felt myself steadily losing consciousness from the pervasively nauseating smell of new and old mothballs. To show my "enthusiasm," I even bought some mothball-smelly clothes for myself, all of which I never wore even after cleaning them. Thrift shop shopping for us was (or so the Girl thought) a shared pursuit and something we could talk about. (My talk usually consisted of asking her, "Aren't you ready to leave the store yet?") It was hard trying to suppress the urge to tell her that some of her get-ups made her look like a seventy-year-old man trapped in a fifteen-year-old body.

It should be noted that for most shared hobbies, there are usually some hidden and not-so-hidden costs, such as dry cleaning bills sizable enough for a parent to consider a second career as a dry cleaning franchisee.

This principle of sharing your child's enthusiasms goes for your teen's new friend he or she is all excited about. Listen well when your teen talks to or about that friend. Teens can get overly enthused about new friends for bad reasons. Encourage your child to bring that new friend around. And then debrief the friend with the skill of an intelligence specialist first class.

– Rule 9 –

Whose body is it, anyway?

I am fortunate that none of my teens ever opted for nose rings, tongue rings, or other things likely to make me lose my lunch, except for the Girl's heavy Addams Family brown lipstick stage and Middle One's brief stint as a bottle blond. Thus, I have been spared some of the more extreme fashion choices that would be the kiss of death to their ever being considered for the Social Register, were they to ever be considered for the Social Register (which was an unlikely prospect. Neither I nor they have ever seen such a book, know anyone in it, or know exactly what it is). I do, however, believe strongly that when a child is a minor, any major changes to the body should be approved (or given the kabosh) before the deed is done. Am I being narrow here? My theory is that if you live in my house, you ask me before you do something rash. It's a control issue. And control is good, if it's the parent that's doing the controlling. If you are in doubt about the need to be firm and unwavering in your stand, think Autocratic State. Think Benevolent Despot. And remember, you and not your teen are the despot.

The one thing parents need to have veto-power over is when their children wish to wear or are wearing something that makes them appear as if they are for-hire by the hour. A parent has the right and obligation to tell the teen to take off or change an outfit that is outrageously lacking fabric where there should be fabric or lacking opacity where body parts require opacity. And if the teens do not heed the call of the parent, preferring to heed the call of the wild, feel free to triple-bolt the front door and lay body across threshold.

To Know: Familiarize Yourself with Puppicks and Toocheses

Any discussion of clothing specifics must start with two principles best explained through two Yiddish words: puppicks (rhymes with *whoop-icks*) and the toocheses (rhymes with *yuch-is-is*). The former phrase refers to the stomach and the surrounding area, including the belly button. The latter phrase, tooches, refers to the rear end of one's anatomy. My theory is that puppicks should not be in public view except in bathing suits at beaches or unless the puppick in question is a puppick of a chicken being served at a meal at my house (in which case, at chicken meals, we say, "Please pass me a puppick," or "Don't eat that. It's the tooches"). By contrast, human toocheses and all parts leading thereto, should not be seen. Period.

Some basic guidelines: if your son's pants fall down without the aid of a belt, they are too big. If any skin shows from the distaff side, namely, your child looks as if she is preparing for a future career in plumbing, that's too little pant and too much skin in view.

If you object to multiple ear or other body-part piercings, you should discuss it with your teen, preferably in advance. (You may want to ask him how he thinks you would look today with ten holes in the ear. But realize that he may offer to pierce your ear in ten places.) If you okay the deed, make sure he goes to a clean, sterile piercing place. This goes for tattoo parlors as well.

– Rule 10 –

Use that important tool in your arsenal: your disappointment and disapproval

Teenagers have a secret life. There are many things your teenagers won't tell you. (And if you have a teenager who tells you each and every thing that happens, that may mean that something may be amiss with you. No offense intended.) If you know the important or bad things that might be happening to your teenager in advance of their happening, you are in good shape. But you also must understand that most of the time, your teenagers are assessing and evaluating their experiences quite without your input. Which means they don't think you are very important in the grand scheme of things. But, in another sense, you're the most important person on your teens' team, even though they would surely attempt to kick you off the team if they knew and understood the part you played.

Your Challenge

So your challenge is this: even though your teens don't spend all that much time with you (read that: they would like to ban you to Planet Krypton for the duration of their teenager-dom), you must still try to be important to them on some level other than for food, money, and rides.

Rarely, your teens may forgo doing some bad thing only because they don't want you to be disappointed big time. But don't count on it. Ideally, your teens should want you to hold them in reasonably high regard. If that's not possible or that's not their goal, they should still want your approval on some level and should still care that if they do certain things, your reaction will pain them in an important irreversible way. This is a subtle but indirect form of social control. And social control is good. Any form of control over your teenager is good. A ball and chain. A leash and muzzle. Threats of banning them to Antarctica or sending them on an extended trip to a nature preserve.

If they're not really interested in pleasing you, you should at least be a Benevolent Despot. And although it feels that your teen shows you zilch love and affection, there is a smidgen that still wants your royal seal of approval and your love. And please don't ask me to quantify how much love and approval she wants from you. You may not want to know.

– Rule 11 –

Choose your battles wisely

This is a hard one. It is important that your teenagers always feel that you care deeply about them and about what they are doing (even when you don't know what they're doing). And they will feel that way only if you are reasonable. Don't get on your teen's case for every little thing. It's counterproductive to building a good relationship. Some pointers:

1) *Make the issue of their room a non-issue.* If there's nothing creepy-crawly in your teens' bedrooms, give up your exasperation about the State of the Room and Closet and try to move on. If your child is amenable to your giving him some mini lessons in organizational skills, try that. But if he wants no part of it, simply try to think of his room as the serf's quarters. (Remember, your house is a fiefdom and you are the Enlightened Despot!) A teen's room is what doors were made for. Teens' clothes are what floors were made for.

2) *The clothing issue shouldn't be an issue.* As long as your teen is dressed for the weather and his pants aren't so low-slung that he could get arrested for indecent exposure, or she will develop pneumonia for having so much cleavage showing, give up that battle for now. If your teen is an average teen (an oxymoron), and even if she's not, she doesn't love the way she looks. Leave your teen alone over the things that won't harm him or his future job or social prospects. Concentrate on the things that count. Is your teen ethical? Is she in the process of developing good judgment? Does he generally and in sketchy outline know right from wrong? Does he know how to choose friends wisely? If you continually carp and express disappointment over every little thing your teenager does, he will consider you to be a disapproving parent, a scold, and an alien with three heads. And then he won't be able to relate to you at all and won't listen to you at times that matter.

3) *The hygiene issue, however, should be an issue.* If your child has hygiene issues or is untidy with his personal appearance, then that's something you do have to deal with. A sudden change in hygiene could mean your child is depressed, on drugs, or very stressed out. Investigate. Act.

Reserve and register your disappointment and disapproval for large things, things that matter. When they do dangerous things. When they don't consider the feelings of others. At that point, don't just act disappointed, do something active and concrete. This way your teen will understand that his error in judgment has consequences, and hopefully he won't repeat it. At least, not right now. Not for the next ten minutes.

To Know

The actual number of stupid things your child could do and has already done and the number of variations of the ones they've done may approach a number so high that mathematicians haven't invented the number yet.

~ Rule 12 ~

Make a plan of action when you're at barf level with your teen: cut him off at the pass

If your child disappoints and frustrates you and makes you approach a state that borders on hatred for your teenager, whatever you do, don't give up. Don't write your child off.

So what's a parent to do? There's one solution that worked for me when I got really, *really* frustrated, and has worked for others I have suggested it to. Think of it as Mini Attitude Adjustment Moment. Or, for want of a better label, I call it Contingency Plan A.

Contingency Plan A: Find That Picture

Find a picture of your child when he or she was a baby or a young child, preferably a photo that you are particularly attached to, the one that keeps following you around from night table to old photo album to dog-eared wallet to your new wallet. Stare at the photo. Stare at it some more. Hopefully, this has the effect of putting your relationship with your child in perspective. Specifically, it should remind you that you love(d) that child fiercely, intensely. Remember that. Remember the sensation you had of hugging that child and of being hugged back (before that child dubbed your kisses "Mommy Slobber"). Remember that cute-looking and cute-acting child? It's the same person. It's that same person you couldn't help but love and who is still that adorable child deep down inside—only where? And how deep down? And will you get the deep-sea bends diving to that point? Then, try once more with feeling to:

Appeal to Your Child's Best Instincts

Which, if he or she doesn't have a drug dependency or a serious mental health issue, may mean asking, What are my child's best instincts? (And yes, they do have them.) They are the feelings your child sometimes has and should have toward you all the time, ideally. Your aim is to get her to treat you the way you deserve to be treated. How do you do this? You appeal to your child's guilt. You start off by saying with great sincerity (which is easy—you are sincere):

The Speech

"You've been treating me badly. You're disrespectful and it hurts my feelings and makes me feel crummy."

Hopefully, this will make her feel sufficiently guilty that she will change her behavior, throw her arms around you, and say, "I'm sorry, Mommy!" But don't count on it. Not right away, anyway. Maybe not this year even. But you will have planted the seeds. And if that doesn't work, go to the next step, which is:

Plan B: The Silent Treatment

If your child doesn't acknowledge that his behavior is wrong, tell your child the following and then stick to it:

The Speech

"Until you decide to be nicer to me, I'm not going to talk to you. At all."

And you can add the following sentence if it fits your feelings:

"In fact, you make me feel so bad, I feel like crying."

If you can cry without the aid of an onion, I'd do that too. Pull out all the stops. But for this occasion, it's got to be real tears. This technique works best when it is not overused. Use it once a year maximum.

The reason Plan B works as well as it does is that it is a practical approach: most teenagers need their parents. For something. A ride somewhere. Your signature for a class trip. Money for a class trip, et cetera. So, therefore, it is profoundly uncomfortable for them to approach you when they realize that you're serious and they need you to do something and it's not happening. The message you are giving them is: they treated you so shabbily, they don't deserve for you to be there for them until they improve their behavior. Give it a few hours, maybe a few days, hopefully not that long. It works—if used sparingly.

~ Rule 13 ~

Don't let your teenagers call you stupid

Every parent should have some baseline behaviors they decide they are not going to tolerate. Stick to these rules and you'll be in better shape than if you didn't. Some cardinal rules:

1) Your teens should not be permitted to call you dumb, stupid, idiot, or any regional variation thereof, or use the words dumb, mental, stupid, or idiot in any sentence that pertains to you. They also cannot call you "psycho-mom" or "psycho-dad," "mental," "nut job," "loon," "loony," or, at random intervals break out into a three-syllable melody: "Loony bin!" (sung with gusto). As stated previously, a family is not a democracy and does not have a bill of rights, and therefore, there is no freedom of speech.

2) Don't let your child curse you out (or "cuss you out" as they say in the South. Or do they?). If they sass you

or curse you, they get punished. End of conversation. And make certain to punish them long enough so that they know you mean business and will punish them if they do it again. Nip it before it buds. Suck it out like poison. And spit it out.

3) Don't let your child slam doors in your face or break doors or walls or destroy property—yours or other people's. If you accept such outbursts, it is only a matter of time until someone gets hurt or hurts himself or also comes into contact with a member of law enforcement who is not the benevolent despot that you are. If your child engages in such behavior, your teen (and you) need help. And the longer such behavior has been going on, the harder it is to get the teen (and possibly you, too) back on track.

4) Don't let your child get physical. Or you with him. Being violent with a teenager gives the (very bad) message that violence is okay in general or okay with family members. A family should have zero violence if for no other reason than you could hurt your child or your child could hurt you. Also, violence has long-term negative consequences for your child, for your relationship with your child, and for society. That is not

to say you should let your child do as he or she pleases. Far from it. There are better disciplinary tactics than getting physical that clearly demonstrate you're in charge and your child cannot do as he pleases.

5) Don't let your child call you by your first name. It's not respectful. You're not his friend, you're his parent. Big difference. Huge. And in some religions, calling one's parent by his or her first name is a big no-no. It's as if your child is saying he or she doesn't have a parent. Which is different than your teen forgetting he has a parent. Which is a natural mistake many teenagers make. If your child persists in calling you by your first name after you've told him it's unacceptable, just don't respond when addressed that way. At all.

∼ Rule 14 ∼

Tell your teen using these exact words: "I am your parent. You are not my social equal"

Whenever I hear a parent say, "My daughter and son are my best friends," I want to choke. Actually, I don't want to choke. To quote Susan Hayward, "I want to live." I want to tell these parents they're wrong. Wrong. Wrong. Wrong. Friends are what your child's peer group consists of. In a family, there are unique and special relationships. You are the parent. They are the teenagers. (It's sort of like, Me Tarzan. You Jane.) And as Rudyard Kipling said, "East is East, and West is West, and never the twain shall meet."

I have few "philosophies" as such about teenagers, but this is one of them: it's bad to aspire to be a "cool parent." However, it's more-than-okay for your children's friends to regard you as "pretty cool" or cute, not because you are, but because you have an open and approachable and appropriately warm way about you, and they therefore like you for those right reasons.

To Know

It is important that your children, and hopefully their friends, respect you for having standards and goals for them and for yourself. It's far better for them to think that you are occasionally unreasonable than for them to think of you as their buddy or their friend.

If you create a relationship of equals between you and your child, why should he listen to you? Does he listen to his friends when his friends tell him what to do? Sometimes. Maybe. Perhaps. Your child won't listen to you if you have that we-are-equal relationship. He won't take you seriously when you are looking to enforce rules or set certain minimum standards of behavior. And why should he if you've given up your parental authority and treat him like a pal?

To put it another way, if it acts like a teenager and walks and talks like a teenager, it probably is a teenager. Be a mom or a dad or be both.

Part of having proper parental authority means saying no, and then after they ask you why, having the right to say, "Because I'm the parent. I don't owe you an explanation." But you can only say this if that's been your attitude all along. And then and only then if you want to, you can explain your reasoning. But that's not the time to do it. You should wait a while. Years.

To Do: Act Your Age

This is not to say that a parent of a teen cannot have a certain amount of youthful *joie de vivre* or that a parent of a teen can't dress youngish or fashionably. What I am saying is a parent should act and look his or her age and not fifteen. And of course, it goes without saying, but I will say it anyway: anyone who is a parent should not take illegal drugs. At all. Period. And a parent who allows underage teenagers to drink at home is wrong, wrong, wrong and does the neighborhood teenagers and their parents a grave disservice.

To Know

There's a downside to sharing your children's clothing.

Moms of female teens shouldn't wear jeans they can't sit down in, even if they have teenager-like bodies. Moms of female teens also shouldn't wear clothes tighter than their girl teens'. Dads of male teens should forgo borrowing their sons' T-shirts unless they have thoroughly read and scrutinized the messages on them, and even then, to be on the safe side, these parents must also possess the skill of advanced cryptographers. Messages contained on teens' T-shirts sometimes have iffy, gross, or hidden messages. Examples include T-shirts' near-religious celebrations of beer drinking till to-vomit-for excess or T-shirts that contain an obscene word that at first glance, looks like a word written in a foreign alphabet. This is known as the obscene T-shirt masquerading as a foreign-alphabet greeting. Do not get taken in by this, or worse, wear the T-shirt in public. (And just a hint: usually, the word contained on the T-shirt is a particularly vile word of Middle English derivation not usually found in standard language dictionaries.)

To Know

You as a parent of a teenager must keep a certain distance from your teen socially. You don't want her to treat you like her friend. And conversely, you don't want to treat teenagers as if they are adults. Try not to share adult things about your life your teens don't need to know. Tell them only as much as they can handle. As your teens approach young adulthood, you can share more details with them. But until that time, give them information in limited doses.

An example (from the pre-pre-pre-teen past): One day, my then-very-young children were riding in my car. Out of the blue, one of them asked me where children came from. I paused (but obviously not long enough), took a deep breath, and launched into a somewhat anatomical and scientific description from my college Biology 101 days. If the reader will pardon the pun, there was a pregnant pause, and then some more pausing, and then a collective response from the backseat: "Yuck!" This is an example of telling your children too much.

Your children and their friends will take you seriously only if you take your role as a parent seriously and are not lazy about it. You can be warm to your children's friends, but don't act like a teenager. You can, and will, develop age-appropriate relationships with their friends (appropriate to both of your ages, that is).

An example: My daughter had two or three friends who were warm, sincere, funny, quality individuals. I adored them. One day, while these girls were visiting, I opened up a piece of mail that had erroneously spelled my name "Fellen Rillberg." This tickled all of us, and we all began laughing hysterically. From then on, my daughter's friends (with my approval) dubbed me "Fellen" and "Fell." Each time they called or came to visit, they would greet me with outstretched arms and would shout, "Fell-en!" It became our little joke. It was an odd but funny way of bonding. But it was an acceptable one. (I had already allowed them to call me by my first name.) Staying close to my daughter's friends had one additional benefit: I could spy on them more easily, if need be.

If your children's friends like and respect you, your child may respect you more.

– Rule 15 –

Don't treat teenagers like mini adults. You need to know more about them than they do about you

Teenagers aren't adults. Teenagers have teenage psyches. They should. They are entitled to. Therefore, try not to talk too much to them about your life or your problems in excruciating detail. Teens should be worrying about school and their social lives and in that order. If your family is having financial difficulties, that's something you can share with your teens. But do it in a way that doesn't cause them to lose sleep unnecessarily.

You also don't want to know everything about your child's social life. What you need to know is:

1) Who their friends are (to assess them, for starters).
2) The negative behaviors they are engaging in, or trying to engage in. (And then act on it promptly.)
3) If they are sexually active.
4) How they are doing in school.
5) If they are reasonably happy. (But if they hum, see 3.)

~ Rule 16 ~

Address the issue of sexual activity with your teens early on— their lives depend upon it

Call me old-fashioned (or don't call me old-fashioned if you agree with me), but I don't think teenagers should be sexually active. At all. But, by the same token, I am also realistic. I realize that if a teenager chooses to be sexually active, he or she must know the dangers and must always use protection. And even then, teens must know that no means of contraception is 100 percent safe or effective. In other words, whatever a parent's view is about teenage sexual activity, at least once early on, the parent must discuss sex with the teenager.

To Do

Parents must explicitly state that to have unprotected sex even once is to play Russian Roulette with one's life. Parents need to also then state that even when condoms are used, there are still risks. Condoms can break or they can be put on too late. Parents should also tell their children that they are not adults and that sexual activity is an adult activity with its attendant emotional and mental risks.

In short: although your viewpoint on teenage sexual activity may be at variance with your teen, you must also realize that you may be the only person over the age of 19 your child interacts with at all who is sensible and who your child has even a passing acquaintance with. And she needs to hear level-headed advice from you. And it is your obligation to both your teen and to those she might intimately encounter to talk about safe sex, even if the thought of your teen having sex makes you want to pull your car over.

~ Rule 17 ~

Teenagers are sneaky—yes, all of them

Some basic knowledge: you are an adult and live in an adult world (or hopefully you do). I am working on the assumption that you don't take drugs except when your doctor prescribes them, do not drink until you are comatose, never drink and drive, and rarely lie. If your teenagers are reasonably normal developmentally, they live in a teenage world. They drink whenever they can. Many teens will try to experiment with alcohol or drugs and, even if they do not drink and drive, they may be tempted at least once to get into a car with another teenager or adult who does drink and drive. And they lie like rugs. So you can see that if you are a responsible adult, you live in a completely different world from teenagers. And those teenagers have one large goal: to avoid detection. Your aim is to try to protect them from slipping into the world of teenagers with bad behavior where they can end up dead, paralyzed, sick, in jail, or just plain unproductive and slipping down the slippery slope of bad behavior.

The Question of the Day is: How do you do this? You develop a network of spies and information-gatherers who have the savvy of a James Bond and the secrecy of Watergate's Deep Throat. As stated previously, you befriend your child's friends' parents as if your child's life depended on it. And it does. Doing this may sometimes be the only way you know where your child is and what your child is doing. If you are fortunate to live in a community that has a group that is addressing the issue of kids and alcohol and kids and drugs, connect with it in some fashion. It will help you. You must address important issues like drinking, drugs, and sex way before they may consider taking part in these activities. But if you find something out after the fact, view it as an opportunity to communicate openly and frankly with your teen about the unsuitability of his behavior.

Something strange happens when children step over that doorway called teendom. Practically all teenagers, including formerly trustworthy, good, honest young people, become sneaky and duplicitous when the need to be that way arises. And their collective aim when they set their minds to it is to dupe their parents into an advanced state of dupedom.

Almost no teens are exempt from this. When they become teenagers, honor students lie. Student leaders lie. All kinds of teenagers lie. This means that you, yes, you, must be prepared to be lied to. And for some parents, if you don't attack this frontally, you must be prepared to be lied to repeatedly, routinely. You'll hear all kinds of lies. White lies. Large untruths. Whoppers. Fish tales. Bald-faced lies. Outrageous equivocations.

To Know: Teens Lie to Their Parents and Sometimes to Their Teachers. Part of Your Job, If Not Your Most Important Function, Is to Catch Them in Their Lies Before the Fact

You must do it for their safety and their well-being. Moreover, if you do not confront your teens when they lie, it sets up the pattern for you to be lied to some more. It also continues to allow them to engage in dangerous behavior undetected. Plus, they may become dishonest adults.

Your chances of catching them in their deception are increased if you enlist their friends' parents, your neighbors, and anyone else who is caring enough to want to help. Teens are counting on parents not sharing to avoid detection.

∼ Rule 18 ∼

If your teen doesn't let you know her whereabouts, hunt her down

It is imperative to keep tabs on your teen's whereabouts. This means that sometimes you have to be prepared to call (many) homes of people you don't know well or at all. Some of the time, your child isn't lying. She just didn't see fit to let you know where she was going. In which case, you will find her.

An example: One time, the Girl left the house for sports practice early on a Saturday morning. When she hadn't surfaced several hours later and I didn't have a clue as to where she was, panic rapidly set in. I began calling each and every one of her friends and teammates until I finally located her at one of her friends' houses.

"My friend's parents think you're weird [she may have used a less flattering term]," she told me, when I finally located her.

"No they don't," I told her. "They probably have done the same thing one time or another." And even if they hadn't, *I didn't care.* I explained to my daughter I didn't care what other parents thought when it came to my child's safety. I also told her that she could have easily avoided the embarrassment by just letting me know where she was going.

The best way to know where your teens are is to bug their rooms and to put secret tracking devices on them—just kidding! The second best way is to ask them where they are going and to check their stories out before they leave, and to track them while they're out. Teens move fast in general, and on an average night, your teen may have been in a handful of places. The third best way to know where they are is to ask your teen's friends' parents where they think their children are. Don't be surprised if each of you thinks your children are at a different place.

When you catch them in lies, punishment should be immediate. Grounding is an especially apt punishment for lying about where they've been.

~ Rule 19 ~

It's good if your children and their friends are afraid of you

It's okay and desirable for your teens and their friends to be afraid of you. This is different from their being terrified of you (a bad thing) or thinking that you don't understand anything. To explain: if your children are afraid of you, meaning that they fear your disappointment or wrath, and that fear will deter them from doing stupid or dangerous things, then that is a good thing. And so be it. And by wrath I do not mean physical force. Teenagers should not be hit or disciplined physically.

Teenagers respect parents who display concern for their kids and who have rules they enforce. Teens definitely do not respect parents who try to act like teenagers or parents who have no rules. Teens also don't respect parents who, word has it, ingest illegal drugs. Teens do respect the parent who is on to them when they are sneaky and up to no good. If teens respect certain parents, those parents can sometimes influence and positively affect teens' behavior. But you can never really know in advance when your influence pays off. So don't count on it.

Question: **So how can I aim to be this respected-parent type?**

Answer: **Try to project an image of someone who is even more savvy, cynical, and cagey than your teen and his friends.**

Stand tall, and wear lifts in your shoes if you are short. If you are small-boned and weak looking, develop some muscles so you look as if you can take on the whole football team, even though you will never lift a finger in physical combat. Part of being a parent and some of the fun requires developing multiple personalities.

If you are worthy of your teen's friends' respect, you will establish relationships with individual friends of your teen throughout the years. Some of these friends may provide some meaningful feedback. However, this requires buttonholing them when they are in your house or on the fly. But you can't count on getting information from these friends on a consistent basis. And they usually won't give you specific information. They may offer an opinion or insight which may or may not be helpful. That's it.

To Know: Your Teen's Friends Won't Tell You What You Need to Know

Don't expect your children's friends or even their teenage siblings to tell you when your teen is in trouble over his head. Teens have a conspiracy of silence. Teens' allegiances are to their fellow teens. That sense of allegiance to other teens is, with rare exception, stronger and more powerful than any other relationship they have, including their relationship with their parents.

Rarely, some older teens may call a parent of a teen who has a drug problem to let the parent know that child is high and out of control. (Or that the child borrowed money from them and didn't pay it back.) But such information cannot be expected.

− Rule 20 −

Make and enforce house rules and out-of-house rules

I have never been a terribly strict parent, but I do have certain rules that seem to work. Most have a common theme and purpose: to not let my home resemble a gerbil cage. To that end, I am strict about these few things:

1) No eating outside the kitchen. Teens are notorious for leaving food-encrusted plates in their rooms buried in places never to be found. This invites creepy crawly things. I have never had trouble with this rule, perhaps because my teens always regarded their rooms as small and low-tech and not worth spending much time in.

2) No dishes in the sink and no dishes left on the kitchen table. My teens knew that if I found dishes in the sink, I would noisily and grumpily put those dirty dishes into the dishwasher whenever I found them (usually before eight o'clock the following morning when I woke up).

If the noise woke them up, that was the price they paid for their slothfulness.

3) No friends over when the parent is not home. It helps to explain to your children the reasoning behind this rule, chiefly that if anything happens while you are away, you could get sued for a gazillion dollars. Somehow your teen understands this explanation, and accepts it without argument.

4) No leaving the house to start the evening at an unreasonably late hour. (And you must tell them what that hour is. Be specific.) If they resist, plant your body along the perimeter of the front door. Generally, they will not opt to peel you off the door unless you are unusually small and frail looking. And even then, they may think twice before attempting to remove you.

5) They must call you to check in, and if you do not answer, they must leave a message that includes a phone number you can reach them at and the name and address of where they are. You will find that they will be slippery. They will call, but if you are not in, they may not leave a phone number. Or they may leave a phone number, but when you call the phone number, they are

not there. Or they may mumble the name of the person so that you can't make out the name. In which case, you may have to enroll them in speech class.

6) If they are staying overnight at a friend's house, there must be a parent present. There have been times when I have asked to speak to the parent whose house my teens were staying at, just to make certain those parents were in fact home and that those parents did in fact exist. Untrusting? You bet. Was my behavior correct? Yes. And necessary.

~ Rule 21 ~

Give your teenagers meaningful chores

When my children were preteens, I developed what I thought was a positively radical parenting theory: I was not going to make taking out the trash my kids' regular responsibility. This was because (in my mind, at least) taking out the garbage was a teeny tiny chore in comparison with other labor-intensive household chores that needed to be done. And I wanted major-league labor contributions. Moreover, taking out the garbage always seemed to be the biggest bone of contention between teenagers and their parents. So, instead, I asked my kids to do a larger, more important task: their laundry. And I schlepped out the garbage and recycling once a week.

Why Laundry?

1) Doing laundry requires a higher degree of responsibility than just taking out the trash.

2) Doing laundry made my teens hate me less than when I did their laundry. Why? I am a bad laundry-doer. I have never learned to sort properly, and I don't have the patience to pick out things that shouldn't be dried in the clothes dryer from things that should. The Girl has two sets of clothes, one that fits her and the other, a set that once fit her but with my (guerrilla laundry) intervention, now fits her Barbie doll. My basic rule of thumb is this: choose your least favorite chore and give it to your teens. Or do that least favorite chore badly and your children will beg to do it for you (e.g., doing laundry).

The Kitchen

Chores in the kitchen include cleaning up directly after eating or after oneself or once friends finish snacking or eating. It should also include pitching in when the family eats as a group (as opposed to each family member eating on her own schedule and grazing and foraging like wild animals). The family that eats together, cleans up together. Remember Snow White and the Seven Dwarfs? Not that I'm comparing the reader to Snow White or teens to the Seven Dwarfs, but the comparison is nonetheless apt. Remember how everybody pitched in and whistled? The job got done. I'm a results-oriented type of person. If my teens resisted clean up, I reminded them that it was a fair deal. I cooked. They cleaned up. And even if I hadn't cooked for them, but instead brought in take-out (which should really be called take-in, but that's another story), they still had to clean up.

If your teens are resistant to this idea, you may want to put their dirty, food-encrusted plates on their pillows. I've never done it, but it's something I've seriously thought about doing.

To Do: Impose Sanctions

If your kids don't do the chores you assigned them, tell them this gives you a bad feeling. If they need an explanation why it gives you a bad feeling, show them the bags under your eyes, the vertical line between your eyes, the swelling of your ankles, or whatever visible sign you have of stress, aging, or general decline. Tell them you work very hard and you are tired and get grumpy when you have to do everything. (See Rule 7 about disapproval and disappointment.) You should also tell them that when they ask you to do something important, you will be less inclined to do it if you feel they are not helpful and are uncaring about your needs. That approach (appealing to their better instincts and practical side) usually works.

71

‒ Rule 22 ‒

Teenagers (and their parents) need curfews

A ll teenagers need curfews. Why?

1) Teenagers aren't parents and thus they don't run their lives. (Or at least they shouldn't think they do; even if they do to an extent, you'd like to think they don't.)

2) Most fatal car accidents occur late at night.

3) Most interactions with police occur late at night.

4) Many interactions with people you don't want your teen interacting with occur late at night. Think phrases such as seedy, soft underbelly, strippers, lap dancers, et cetera.

5) The later a teen stays out, the greater the chance is that the teen will get into trouble. An equation: too much time without parental interface equals negative teen action and behavior. Remember *West Side Story?* If Riff had stayed in the grocery store and the Sharks and the Jets hadn't had so much time to rumble in the handball

courts and hang out in the playgrounds, there wouldn't have been a West Side Story. Ditto for Romeo and Juliet.

As to what the curfew should be: for younger teenagers, something between 10:00 and 11:00 P.M. on the weekends may not be too late. For older teenagers, start at 12:00 or 12:30 and hold firm for as long as you can. When in doubt, talk to other parents and find out what their teens' curfews are. But choose a curfew that you—and your sleep-deprived body—can live with.

What To Do If Your Child Breaks Curfew

If your non-driving teen tells you the getting-home part is the problem, tell him he should call you. If he calls and says he will be 5 to 15 minutes late, that's okay, generally. You don't want some inexperienced driver with barely passable driving skills (i.e., some other teen) speeding to bring your teen home. (Although that driver may be speeding because that's what many teen drivers do.)

If your teen is routinely late getting home, then there must be a consequence such as grounding or drawing and quartering them, metaphorically speaking.

Question: **How do you know if the curfew you've chosen is correct?**

Answer: **Talk to other parents you respect if you're not certain what the curfew for your teenager ought to be.**

Chances are, you will find that not all parents impose the same curfew and that generally, kids who have earlier curfews abide by them. Moreover, friends of the teen with the earlier curfew make certain their friend doesn't blow his curfew. If your child wants you to raise the curfew, think before you do. Perhaps you can raise it on a trial basis or for special occasions only.

To Know: If Your Child Begins the Night with One Friend or a Set of Friends but Ends with Another Friend or Set of Friends, His or Her Curfew Is Too Late

If the kids your teen started the evening with are already at home, that means that those teens had earlier curfews than your child, or they didn't approve of the activity your child ended up doing. The hallmark of a teen is that he doesn't always exercise good judgment. Add fatigue, liquor, and new characters who are more objectionable to you than the first crew of friends he started the evening out with, and there shouldn't be that second half of the evening with those new characters.

~ Rule 23 ~

Let the school know you

It is important to be involved in your child's school. This can sometimes be very hard if you work long hours or hold down more than one job. It can also be uncomfortable for you if you were a poor student and are allergic to the sight of schools.

Why be involved?

1) If school personnel know you, they will more likely pay special attention to your child and will let you know when there are problems before those problems become Milky-Way large. If you are involved in the school, school personnel regard you as part of the community. The school may also come to regard you as a responsible parent only because you are known (in which case, it's almost irrelevant whether you really are a good or responsible parent). I have no hard statistics on this, but I believe school personnel are more likely to pick up the phone to call parents they know

if for no other reason than they regard those parents as known quantities.

2) Human nature being what it is, if you offer to help the school, school personnel will like you. If you have bought into the concept that it pays to be an involved parent, you must first figure out what it is you can contribute. Do you speak a foreign language? Offer to speak to foreign language classes during Foreign Language Week. If you know how to build something or paint and the kids have a carnival or some big project coming up, offer your help. Let the school know what skills you possess.

If your children play sports, join the Booster Club and go to all the football games. (And you can do that even if you don't have a child who plays sports.) Join the PTA. Support their activities. Bake for them if your baked goods will not make people sick. If you work full time, on the rare day when you are home and school is in session, try to stop by the school even if it is simply to drop a book off just so the school will know your face. It doesn't matter what your face looks like except that you must slap a smile on it and try not to look like a misfit.

And of course, go to Open School Night and take notes. Learn what the teachers' expectations are. Don't expect to understand everything the teacher says, especially if your child studies a foreign language you haven't studied. And your eyes may glaze over when their math and science teachers start throwing out math and science terms like neutrinos, quarks, and algorithms, unless you have a higher degree in math and science. Simply nod your head at appropriate intervals. Nodding your head vigorously may also help you to stay awake, in the event one of the teachers has a sleep-inducing voice that drones on and on. And at least one teacher does. (Zzzzzzz.)

Just so you know, Open School Night is not the time for you to take up with the teacher any problem your child might have, especially when there is a line several dozen parents thick waiting to introduce themselves to the teacher. You can do that during parent-teacher conference time or by calling the teacher at some other time that is mutually convenient.

To Know

Generally, if you call a teacher, that is a good thing. If a teacher calls you, that is a bad thing. Teachers tend to call to convey unpleasant news or to ask, "Do you own a dog?" As in your kid said the dog ate your kid's homework.

~ Rule 24 ~

If you hear from your teen's teachers, call them back immediately

If you want your child to do well in school, you must embrace the principle that teachers are partners with parents, and vice versa. And even when you think that partner fell short of your idea of terrific or even average, you must not get obnoxious or accusatory with that teacher. Not right away, anyway, with some notable exceptions.

To Know

There are two sides to every story: the teacher's and the student's. Or possibly a third side, something in the middle. Listen to both sides of the story and consider that there may be that middle version, but that's usually not the case.

Most school problems are attitudinal—your teen's attitude, that is. It also helps to know that no one loves a wisenheimer, especially a teacher. The wisenheimer has the ability to make other students laugh (and teachers like to feel they are the only comedians even if they have zilch sense of humor). So, if you get a call from a teacher and you're not home, assume it's about your child's bad attitude or lack of motivation, and get on the stick that very day and call that teacher back, making certain to leave several contact numbers if you're hard to reach. And try to sound cheerful, even if you are not having cheery thoughts about your child.

To Know

If the teacher took the time to call, it generally means that something is wrong. And usually the amount of wrong is not just a little bit wrong.

To Know: Start with the Teacher and Work Your Way Up, If Need Be

When you do make contact, let the teacher know straight out that you support his or her authority and that you won't tolerate your child being fresh—if that's what the teacher called to tell you. If the teacher is calling to tell you your child is being lazy and may flunk a subject, then that's something different. But both messages require that you spring into action.

To Do: Develop a Game Plan

Establish a schedule of contact with the teacher from now until the end of the school year and stick to it. Calling is better than writing. A sneaky student may intercept a letter in the mail. If things are critical, arrange to go to the school and meet the teacher face to face. And continue to meet with the teacher multiple times. If the problem is both attitudinal and academic (i.e., he may flunk unless he shapes up), let the teacher do most of the talking. Let the teacher tell you exactly what needs to be handed in and when—the exact due dates. Let the teacher tell you how your teen's bad attitude manifests itself, so you have a clear picture (this may result in your blood pressure rising, but at least you can attack the problem armed, but not with anything dangerous in your hand, that is).

To Do: Diagnose the Problem

If the problem is one of attitude, namely the child was fresh to the teacher, then punishment such as grounding or loss of phone privileges is in order. And it is important to stress to your teenager that if he is college-bound (and even if he's not), the last thing he wants in his file are letters or formal documents citing discipline problems. You must also consider that if your child has a history of not obeying authority figures, therapy or counseling is in order.

Question: **What do you do if you think the teacher is wrong?**

Answer: **Tread carefully before acting.**

And ask yourself whether the teacher did something significant enough that you want to take it up with the department head, or perhaps someone higher. But understand: I am not saying you should not contact school officials if a teacher has done something unethical, immoral, or out-there. I'm saying you should try to be armed with an accurate account of events from your child. And in most cases, you should be prepared to hear the teacher out and start with the teacher and work your way up the chain of command in the school, if need be. However, in cases where a teacher is behaving in a clearly and seriously unacceptable way, you must proceed around the teacher. Speak to school authorities, and if there is criminal conduct involved, contact the appropriate authorities or the police.

For less serious problems, it is almost never a good idea to take the approach that your child is 100 percent right and the teacher is 100 percent wrong. Once you have the facts, you can try to appeal to the teacher's better instincts, especially if the teacher is in the wrong.

An example (this occurred when the Girl was a preteen): One day my daughter came home from school very upset. She told me that her teacher didn't like her and was treating her mean. I sprang into action: I set up a meeting with the teacher. In a non-accusatory manner, I told the teacher that my child felt bad because she felt the teacher did not like her. The teacher was shocked and felt terrible. She insisted she did like my daughter. So where did my daughter get this from? The teacher was due to retire at the end of the year and she was grumpy in general, possibly to everyone. (Perhaps she directed her anger at some of the more active, involved members of the class.)

The lesson of this story: following the meeting, the teacher began treating my daughter better. Had I gone up to the meeting with a you-have-some-nerve-treating-my-daughter-mean attitude, the result would likely not have been as positive.

The flip side is when the child is at fault.

An example: Once I got a call from Middle One's teacher. He was a brand-new teacher. He told me Middle One was disrespectful in class. I immediately let the teacher know that the teacher was right, my child was wrong, and I was prepared to nip it in the bud. I told the teacher I would speak to my child. We agreed that the teacher and I would speak at least once a week to see how things were going. During at least one of those phone conversations, I learned that things weren't going well enough. I put the screws on. I made sure my son shaped up.

~ Rule 25 ~

Regard beer and hard liquor as the unseen enemy

The great philosopher Descartes said, "I think, therefore I am." Teenagers are not that advanced. Their manifesto (if they had one) would be, "I drink, therefore I am." They don't understand risks, even if they are taught those dangers in health class or even if one of their friends is paralyzed or dies from an alcohol-related occurrence.

To Know

Beer and hard liquor are everywhere. And it is the parent's job to find the alcohol, ferret it out, and extirpate it. Most teens drink, and many teens drink to excess. Teens whose parents think their kids don't drink, drink. Parents who think their children drink recreationally probably don't know what their child's version of recreational is. If they are allowed to, teenagers and preteens will drink in parks, on the street, in the street, on roofs, in deserted houses, in houses without parental supervision, in the ocean, pools, ponds, and rivers, to name only a few.

Teens will also drink in houses where parents allow them to. Those parents mistakenly justify their conduct by saying that it is safer to let kids drink with a roof over their heads, meaning their roof. Which is one more reason why it is important to speak to other parents of teenagers, especially parents whose houses your teens visit. You must find out other parents' views on things such as beer, marijuana, smoking, and orgies.

Parents of teenagers either develop (or are naturally equipped with) a built-in beer detector. I once found a six-pack outside under a pile of pine needles hidden in the catch area of my outside basement window. How did I find it? Something just told me to go outside and look around my house.

If you doubt this, or if you just want to know how important drinking is to your child, find out where your teen has hidden his junior high or high school yearbook. You may find entries such as the following: "Remember when we drank the scotch in your mother's liquor cabinet?" (And that's a tame entry.) If you have a teenager and there is alcohol anywhere in your house, they and their friends will find it. And if it's not in your house, they will obtain it.

To Repeat

Alcohol is one of the largest perils your children will face. Chances are that your teen will drink to excess at least once and probably more than once. And even though teens may have been taught in school or told by you that binge drinking or drinking to excess can result in death or serious injury, that will not deter some of them from ending up in your local hospital or morgue. And unfortunately, many parents remain blind to the threat.

An example: One night while waiting for the Girl's sports injury to be treated in the emergency room, I met two sets of parents who had children in high school. One parent told me his teenager fell down a flight of stairs while drunk and that it was the second such incident in a brief period of time. The other boy was comatose from binge-drinking—he later recovered. The odd thing was, when I ran into the parents of the comatose student, they minimized the seriousness of the incident. To hear them tell it, it was as if he got a scratch on his elbow.

To Know: If Your Teen Drinks to Excess, He Will Continue to Do So Unless Someone or Something Intervenes

If teens drink in middle school and high school, as so many of them do, they surely don't quit drinking once they go off to college (and are no longer subject to their parents' daily scrutiny). If they have a drinking problem, it only gets worse with time. Unlike drug use, alcohol use and misuse is not always visible on your teen's body or face. If your teen has barfed after drinking, the following morning he might look just fine—once he wakes up, that is.

To Do

Acknowledge the problem early on. If your child gets so drunk even once that she does not know what she is doing, insist on alcohol counseling and/or psychological counseling and stick to your demand.

Compounding the problem is that most teenagers (and adults for that matter) who have problems with alcohol deny the problem or erroneously believe that they can handle it themselves. They promise not to drink and sometimes adhere to the policy—until the next slip-up. So what can you do? If you are fortunate enough to have a support group of parents who band together to address the problem, join the group or go to their meetings, or at the very least, talk to the organizers of the group. Obtain their literature. Involve yourself. You will learn where the kids do their drinking and what you can do to deter the drinking. You will start to talk to other parents your children are with, and you can strategize together.

Teens spend a good deal of energy trying to find houses where the parents are away for the weekend. Their aim: to have a party there. Teens also have special places they go to drink, usually deserted areas where it is hard to find them. If you can find out where such a place is, talk to other parents about it. And act.

Last, you must look long and hard at yourself and your own alcohol consumption (if you drink at all). And ask yourself: do you drink in front of your kids, and if you do, how often?

– Rule 26 –

Your teen will try to throw at least one party when you are not home (ever seen *Risky Business?*)

To avoid having your teens throw a party when you are not home, you can:

1) Never leave your home.

2) Take your teens with you whenever you leave town. Trust no one. Take no prisoners. Except your teenagers.

3) If your teens are staying with other families, you might consider giving the adults a pair of reins to be used on your children not unlike the kind used fifty years ago by parents of little children with severe cases of wanderlust (only now the teen-children have less wander and more lust).

A painful example: The Girl and Middle One threw a party while my husband and I went to visit Big Boy during his college's Parents' Weekend. Since it was a monotonous eight-hour drive, we devised what we thought was a well-thought-out plan: leave the two younger teens with Grandma, who is a smart, youthful, and on-the-ball grandmother (almost all the time). The plan was that Grandma would pick up the Girl and Middle One after school and would then drive them to her house, where they would stay and sleep. Middle One had his own well-thought-out plan. He told his sister to tell Grandma that she would prefer sleeping at her friend's house. Middle One told Grandma that he also would prefer to sleep at his friend's house, and that he made the appropriate plans. For some reason I'm not sure of (Grandma trusted them, maybe?), Grandma bought their stories. That night, when I called Grandma's house and she didn't answer, I just assumed she was en route back to her house with the kids and was running late. So my husband and I had no idea what was happening—which was that the two kids threw a party, and both kids slept in our empty home. Each of them invited a same-gender friend as company. Hopefully, they didn't play musical rooms.

To Do: Catch Them in the Act, or in the Immediate Aftermath

When I got home from the visit to Big Boy's college, I went to the basement to do a routine chore and noticed a window was open. It was opened wide enough that anyone who wanted to could have entered the house. That worried me, because I never open those windows. I asked my kids why the window was opened and I don't remember what they told me, but their explanations didn't make sense. And then the phone rang. It was one of my son's friends' mothers. She told me her son returned home drunk the previous night and that she finally squeezed out of him that he had been at a party at my house. She asked me if I knew about the party. I don't remember the rest of our conversation (I was seeing all kinds of colors). I may have told her that my kids were dead meat.

I thanked the mother profusely for informing me, after inquiring whether her son was okay—thank goodness, he was. I then decided to ask my kids some more questions about the Open Window, not letting on that I knew anything—a little squirming would be productive, I felt. I spoke to each child separately. (A military image: divide and conquer!) I asked each child why brother and sister had stayed at friends' houses instead of staying with Grandma as we had arranged. Little by little, the seams in the story split open. The Girl was far more contrite than Middle One, who felt worse about being caught than about what he had done. The Girl burst out crying when the real story eventually came out. I told her she had destroyed the considerable amount of trust I had had in her. Middle One rose to his sister's defense and told me it was all his doing and that he had twisted her arm to get her to lie to Grandma. (I checked for twist marks on her arm and found none.) Grandma was understandably furious about being duped. Point of fact: I don't think she ever forgave Middle One.

Result: the kids were grounded for a long time, and I didn't permit them to use the phone. And there were other deprivations. No video games. No radio. No television. In short, they learned a lesson. Until the next time they were sneaky and lied to me. But they never again threw a party without my being there.

– Rule 27 –

If you really want to know what your teens are up to, you must snoop on even the best of them

I recently visited a store that carried all the high-tech and low-tech and in-between-tech items necessary to spy on whatever one must spy on. I could have used some of the tools of that trade several years ago. Not to mention, I have always wanted to walk around in my secret life saying, "Jane. Jane Bond."

To Know: There's a Difference Between Privacy and Respecting a Teen's Person and Personal Space

I'm a firm believer in respecting a teenager's person. I never walked in on my teens without knocking, and I always waited for them to tell me I could come in. As for their right to privacy, I say: What right? Teenagers live in their parents' or guardians' house. Returning to our Middle Ages imagery, remember, your teens are the serfs. You are the landowners.

Serfs don't own the land. And your teen-serfs live mostly rent-free.

To Know

Teens live a secret life to a certain extent. To the extent that the secret part is not dangerous, you don't have to know about it. To the extent that it is potentially dangerous, you must try to find out about it and work to protect your child against it. Remember that teens' judgment is impaired or nonexistent. And while they may know what is the right thing to do and what is not the right thing to do, they may not do the right thing. They may do just the opposite. More likely than not, they will do the wrong thing.

So, what's a parent to do? If you are worried about your child, you look in their drawers and closets and anywhere they can secrete objects. You read letters. You search for signs of drugs or sexual activity, not necessarily because you think they are drug users or non-virgins but because to not know whatever it is that is out there will be worse for you and your teen in the long run. It is during these forays that you may find all kinds of important things.

If your children are sexually active, you must know. If you discover any signs of drug use such as marijuana, pipes, rolling paper, or other drug paraphernalia (some of which you wouldn't even know what it was unless you've done some reading or have been shown some pictures of drug paraphernalia at a community forum or elsewhere), you cannot afford to ignore it.

The following is a partial list of what parents might find in their teens' drawers:

1) Notes, usually from members of the opposite sex, about past or future sexual trysts.

2) Notes with terms or phrases you are unfamiliar with but which sound as if they could only have one meaning related to sex, drugs, or rock and roll, such as "hooked up with" (and the school is not performing "Peter Pan").

3) Notes with terms that you are familiar with, but not totally familiar with, such as "bongs" or anything referring to weights and measures such as "kilos" (unless of course you live in a country that uses the metric system).

4) Official letters from school addressed to you that you never saw, usually with dates so stale that the print is flaking off the paper.

5) Papers with words in capital letters and papers of weird sizes, shapes, or colors. This includes court

appearances, appearance tickets, or ticket-tickets (which even if they have information about responding by mail, if they are not responded to, might result in visits to court or possibly jail time).

6) Condoms or other forms of birth control. (If you are not current on all the forms of birth control out there, look for objects that resemble miniature flying saucers, pills that are small, pills that are horse-sized, and anything else that may look like something other than what it is.

7) Illicit substances or anything in a package or lying loose that you're not sure what it is. This could be liquid or solid, strawlike, or brightly colored. It could look like something you might eat something with but wouldn't, such as a spoon that is not spoon-sized, or something spoon-sized.

8) Bills from doctors whose names you are not familiar with who specialize in (private) parts of the body containing diagnoses that cause you to run to the dictionary or cause you to hyperventilate.

9) Emergency room bills or aftercare slips.

10) Photos of your teens or possibly other teens whom you've never seen before but who obviously were with your teen during the photo-taking session, whose slumping bodies resemble limp pieces of spinach and

whose smiles look unnaturally happy or their eyes, unnaturally small.

11) Photos of your teen or friends of your teen wearing underwear or not wearing underwear or wearing underwear on places not normally associated with underwear (on their heads) or turning their backs to the camera while wearing underwear and then performing an anti-gravitational gesture with the underwear, not sanctioned in etiquette books.

Finding any of the above should lead you to the conclusion that you really don't know your teen well enough. This list, while not exhaustive, should convince parents that what parents need to know, they don't and won't know if their teenagers can help it. Your teen's aim is to suppress the information flow, and yours is to make it flow like the Mississippi River after a flood.

– Rule 28 –

Your teens need to work and need guidance in their choice of work

If your child isn't president of the school and playing three varsity sports throughout the year or volunteering loads of time to worthwhile projects, your child needs a job. (And he still might need a job. But he may not have any hours left for work.) Why?

1) A job gives your child a needed sense of responsibility, both financial and otherwise. At work, your child will learn to show up on time, have clean clothes or a uniform at all times, and adhere to standards set by someone other than a teacher or family member. He will join the market economy. He will receive a paycheck. He will have taxes deducted. And maybe, he will no longer relate to his parent as a human Fort Knox.

2) A job teaches your child time management. Most teenagers have some free time. Most schools have an instructional day of less than six hours. Even with

after-school activities, that leaves a large chunk of time to be used in negative or nonproductive ways (one of which is reproductive ways, which is not good). And human nature being what it is (and teen human nature being what it is), most of that time won't be spent doing homework, unless your child aims to be valedictorian. The more time your children have on their hands, the greater the likelihood that they will either fritter the time away or get into trouble—or both. This is not a reflection on your teenager specifically. It is a reflection of human nature. To put it another way: free time is your enemy and your teenager's.

Types of jobs teens should hold

Part of the purpose of a first job is to introduce the teen to the world of work and to make that first experience a positive one so that your teen won't set as his next goal retirement at age sixteen or of landing a rich future mate. Generally speaking, I like large supermarkets or fast-food restaurants as first jobs because those kinds of establishments are accustomed to training large numbers of first-time workers. Also, those kinds of workplaces have clear rules, standards, and expectations that (hopefully) are laid out for the teen.

– Rule 29 –

Your child should work at a safe place

This may seem obvious, but it's not. Just because a workplace is part of a national chain does not mean that it follows all of the wage and hours laws or child labor laws scrupulously. Check to see whether a potential employer has gotten cited for unsafe working conditions. Check for a policy that requires parental written permission if a child works later than a certain hour on a school night, and then decide if you want to sign off on it. Don't sign if you feel your child will be too tired for school the next morning. Teens are notoriously sleep deprived. You don't want your teen working at a job that demands too many hours or too-late hours. Places that have rats are a no-no, as are places that use dangerous equipment. How do you know a place has rats? Your child may tell you, or you may be able to guess, if the rear of the building contains poorly contained refuse (or if you or your child see rodent droppings. Been there. Done that).

Some things to consider when helping your teen decide whether to work at a large or small company:

At large companies:

1) They sometimes offer scholarships for college.
2) They may be able to accommodate exam schedules and special events because they have a larger number of employees. (But then again, they may be short staffed, or if they are a retail store and Christmas is their big season, they may put unreasonable time demands on your teen at times your teen needs to study more and work less.)
3) They may have a union that could give your child additional coverage your own policy doesn't have, like a dental plan or eyeglasses.
4) If the employer observes wage and hours laws and other work rules, they won't ask your child to work times and hours she shouldn't.

At small companies:

1) Your child may have a closer relationship to the employer, and if your child is a self-starter, she may be able to use certain skills and aptitudes that she couldn't use at a larger place.
2) Your child may find a job that matches his knowledge base, for example, working at a store that sells comic books if his hobby has been comic book collecting or reading. By the same token, if your child spends much

of his paycheck on those comic books or whatever product it is the employer sells, that may not be such a wise place to work.

3) The employer may be more accommodating about your child's school needs.

– Rule 30 –

Encourage sports participation unless your teen has two left feet

Iam a firm believer that most teenagers benefit from being involved in an organized sports program. They learn how to be team players both on the field and off. They learn how to take advice and criticism or else get benched or chucked from the team. They share in their team's victories. They learn about disappointments and how to deal with them, such as when they don't get much playing time or don't get to play at all. (In which case, they may not get much exercise value from their sport, except during practice.)

They also shower regularly. (Or else, they reek and their teammates will hate them after the game is over.) They learn about six-pack stomachs (as opposed to six packs in the stomach).

Sports participation also allows your teen to enlarge her circle of friends while simultaneously developing skills and a level of fitness she would not otherwise have.

Another significant benefit: having a child on a sports team allows a working parent to know where the teen is each day between the end of the school day and 6:00 or 7:00 P.M. And it is better to know your teen is on a playing field than getting friendly with a member of the opposite sex in your house when no one is there. Or hanging out. Or contemplating her navel or any other part of her body. Additionally, students who participate in sports throughout the school year learn to manage their time better than students who have a lot of free time.

To Know: It Isn't Necessary That Your Child Excel At Any Given Sport

Don't assume your child must be talented, or even very athletic, to play a sport (unless of course your school's teams are so great that only the super-duper players get chosen or get any playing time). Middle One was very small for most of his teen years, and try as he might, he only got 30 seconds of playing time his first season of football. Did he regret being a member of the team? No. The Girl played lacrosse, basketball, and volleyball each season. She was a passable basketball player, an above-average volleyball player, and a good lacrosse player, but that didn't stop her from playing all three sports each season and enjoying it. Being a member of a sports team also gives students the opportunity to work their way up the ranks and develop leadership skills so that by the time they are seniors in high school, they can become team captains or co-captains.

Even if your teen has no leadership ability, simply being a team member teaches discipline and the ability to understand what "You're a team player" means on and off the field in later life.

To Know: Sports Participation Can Sometimes Help Your Teen Get into the College of Her Choice (Even If She Doesn't Play on the College Team)

There are many colleges that will accept a student because that student played a sport, but at the same time, the college does not impose an obligation for the student to play that sport once the student gets into that school. Most colleges view high school sports participation as a plus. And these days, students need lots of pluses to get into the colleges of their choice.

As to the virtues of girls' sports participation, more than one study has shown that girls who engage in sports have better self-esteem and a healthier view of their bodies than girls who do not play sports. And being on sports teams can teach girls how to compete.

– Rule 31 –

To buy a car or not to buy a car, that is the question—not!

To Not Do

Don't buy your teen a car even if you can afford it. Let the teen earn the car. I have met too many parents who bought their child a car, only to have it totaled almost immediately. Because the child knows he or she did not earn the car, he is not as careful with it than if he had earned it. It has been my experience that almost all the kids who earned the money to purchase their cars did not get into accidents with their cars.

The same principle inheres with all manner of traffic tickets: you must make your children pay for them. You must teach your children that negative conduct has consequences for which they, and not you, are economically responsible.

If you have even a remote suspicion that your child gets behind the wheel after drinking, take the keys and all the duplicate keys away permanently and punish him. And seek help.

— Rule 32 —

Subsidize your teen at your peril

There are some families whose teens pay most of their own way. These teens work and pay for their own clothes and incidentals and save up money for a car and car insurance. Then there are other parents who pay for part of their teens' expenses. There is the third set of parents who make no financial demands on their teens and do not think that teenagers should work. This last group generally produces the monster known as the Give-Me Do-For-Me teen. These teens have a never-ending set of material requests, and their parents seemingly have an inexhaustible monetary reserve to satisfy their children's every need (or else they have a misguided impulse which they characterize as self-sacrifice). These parents spoil their teens rotten. These teens expect things from their parents endlessly. And once they receive what they have demanded, the teens do not appreciate it and demand even more money and things. Your aim is to encourage your children not to be friends with such children, and certainly your aim should be not to produce such children.

An example: A fourteen-year-old wanted to attend a local summer camp. The parent felt the summer camp tuition was excessive. Moreover, there were other, more moderately priced summer camps in the neighborhood that the girl could have easily attended, but the teen was adamant: she wanted to go to that summer camp and that one only. I suggested that the parent ask the daughter to pay for one-half of the camp's tuition. I then suggested she ask her teenager to sign a contract stating that she would pay for the other half of the tuition by working. Did the child feel put-upon? Yes, but this action set a new course for this family. By asking the teen to assume one-half of the financial responsibility, the parents were beginning to carve out new roles for themselves and their daughter.

When parents subsidize their teens endlessly, the teens find it a rude transition into the world of financial independence later on. Or they don't make the transition. This is a private form of welfare. I call it Parentfare or Mommy-and-Daddyfare.

~ Rule 33 ~

Encourage your teen to be a joiner

U nless your child has to work long hours because of family financial necessity, most teens have time to belong to after-school groups and other worthwhile community organizations. And they should. Your child will develop skills and may discover talents she didn't even know she had. Or even if your teen thought she had some skill or aptitude, that sense will be encouraged and hopefully will be borne out by the faculty advisor, whose aim is to encourage everyone and not just the superstars.

To Do: Help Your Child Pick Her Activities

What kind of activities should your teen join? Generally, there are three kinds of school-based after-school clubs. One is academic and interest-related clubs, such as the Spanish club or the psychology club. These clubs help develop an interest the student has in a given field. Next, there are service clubs that visit nursing homes or raise money for charities that may or may not be linked to a larger national organization. There is also a third set of clubs that feed into other, larger, regional or national entities, such as Model United Nations, Moot Court, or Forensics. The latter groups generally have a large project that the students work on for a portion of the year that often culminates in some kind of regional competition. The virtue of this latter kind of club is that your school will be given materials that are generally very polished and professional and that have been worked on by a large group of people devoted to that task (which is something an independent club would not necessarily have). There is real excitement to these competitions.

Membership in any of these activities enlarges your children's circle of friends and associates. In clubs, friendships among the students are forged based on a shared interest. If your school does not have any of these clubs, consider approaching the principal and trying to start one.

An example: My children's school did not have a debating club or a Forensics Club, which is a national debate society. I contacted the Forensics advisor at a nearby high school to find out about the club (which I knew very little about). I found out how the club operated and how it fed into the larger national organization. Then I approached the high school principal at my children's school, who found both a faculty advisor and a budget line for the club. One weekend, the faculty advisor and

I went to see a nearby countywide competition. Lesson: we started the club at my children's high school. Did my kids then join the club? No. They had no interest. Was I sorry I invested time and energy into getting the club started? No. Other kids will benefit, and that's the good thing.

Another large advantage to joining a club that has some sort of competition or test of your child's skill is that it may help to get them into college.

Where I live, all the singers and kids who play musical instruments participate in a competition that starts at the county level and continues to the state level and beyond. The kids take a test individually. If they score high enough, they are asked to compete in a large concert held in a large impressive concert hall. Thousands of people attend.

Even if your child doesn't opt to join any of the larger clubs, sometimes a teacher will recognize a child's talent and try to help cultivate it.

An example: Although Big Boy had a wonderful singing voice, he had only started to sing in his junior year of high school and thus, his sight reading was deficient. Even though he received a high voice rating, he didn't advance to the county competition level because of his poor sightreading skills. Big Boy's teacher liked his voice so much, he arranged for my son to get free individual lessons at a local music college.

Unfortunately, my son didn't love one-on-one voice lessons, and after three such free lessons (and after the teacher told me he had a voice like Michael Crawford's), he quit. Which leads to Lesson Number Two: teach your teen to stick it out, whatever the "it" is.

To Know: If You Allow Your Teen to Quit Things, You Are Teaching Your Child to Be a Quitter

It's important to teach your child that to be successful in life, he must learn to persist and persevere even when it's unpleasant and uncomfortable.

An example: One year, the Girl decided she didn't want to play basketball. It was mid-season; she was getting next-to-no playing time and she was miserable. We talked it over. I asked her if maybe it would be a better idea to finish out the season with her team. She said no. She was firm about it. And she wasn't normally a quitter. I asked her father what he thought about it. He told me and then he told my daughter and then we told her together that it was a bad life lesson to drop something in the middle. He told her that by joining a team, she had tacitly agreed to stay the whole season and that it would be wrong to leave. And so she stayed. Reluctantly? Somewhat. But she knew and I knew he was right. The fact was, there wasn't a good-enough reason for my daughter to quit. While she arguably wasn't being treated entirely fairly—some players who were on her level got more playing time than she did—she wasn't being treated grossly unfairly.

To Know: Recognize the Deja Vu's If Your Aim Is to Produce a Much-improved Version of Yourself

Many years ago, I was chosen for an advanced Spanish course that was really difficult. I felt I didn't belong there. I felt pressured. I begged my mother to let me move to the less-demanding middle track. My mother spoke to the teacher, who balked at her request. He told my mother I belonged in the advanced class. My mother and I insisted that I be permitted to leave the accelerated class. I was permitted. The following year, I had the bad fortune of getting that same teacher, and he hadn't forgotten that I had left his advanced class against his advice. Moreover, he had one very large drawback as a teacher: he had a cruel streak. He decided it was payback time. He gave me an insulting nickname, and that's all he called me that entire year. Of course it was wrong for him to give me that nickname, but apart from that, it was also wrong for me and my mother to have let me bail.

~ Rule 34 ~

Notice if your child is in trouble

If your teen is more quiet than normal, it could be that he is in trouble or troubled. Generally, in trouble means he did something for which there have already been unpleasant consequences that you are clueless about. Troubled, on the other hand, means there has been a series of things he did that you also are unaware of that troubles your teen, something that may or may not have already gotten him into trouble. All of the above should be troubling to you if (to quote Peter Lorre) you know nothing (and badly need to know something).

To Know

Your aim is to know precisely the thing your teen doesn't want you to know. Think of your task as that of a top-notch wartime cryptographer. Crack that code. Figure out the mind-set of your teen without going batty.

Your task is compounded by the fact that if your teen is into the in-trouble or troubled mode, chances are he will be heavily into a parent-avoidance mode. You can spot this mode by his shifty eyes and the accelerated rate of speed and body propulsion when he leaves the house. At times like this, his body is not unlike that of a speeding bullet.

Some things your child may not tell you (particularly if he's an older teen):

1) That he's gotten into trouble at school;
2) That he's about to fail a subject or subjects;
3) That he's in trouble with the law;
4) That he's had a car accident or has done something bad to another person or someone's property;
5) That he's gotten fired from his job.

An example: I once got a call from one of my son's college roommates. Although I didn't know him well, he sounded troubled. He asked me if I knew how to get a wrecked car to an auto body store. I asked him why he wanted to know that. He said that while he was driving on the highway, a driver cut him off. Although no one had been injured, his parents' car was totaled. I asked him if his parents knew. He said no, that they were on vacation and he did not want to ruin their vacation. I told him he had to call them up and tell them what happened. (In short, if I hadn't told him to call his parents, he wouldn't have.)

Some Warning Signs of Trouble

1) Weight loss or weight gain that doesn't correspond to normal growth. This could be a sign of depression. It

could also be a sign of an eating disorder. Eating disorders have become increasingly prevalent among teens, and it is at near-epidemic proportions in some communities. If you're on the heavy side and your child is suddenly plumping up, it could just mean that Mother Nature kicked in and your child has your easily-gains-weight gene. Which for health reasons, should concern you.

2) Tiredness. This too could be a sign of depression or drug use. It could also just mean that your teen is oversubscribed in school, sports, social life, or any combination from A, B, or C. Teens are notoriously oversubscribed. To not be oversubscribed and to have time to contemplate one's navel or nose ring is to be a geek by teen standards.

3) A sudden change in school performance. Same as above.

4) A change in routine. If your child always played sports and suddenly doesn't want to play, explore why. If your teen is suddenly staying home more often or if your teen is being too nice to you, question it. Never consider kindness and consideration normal in your teen unless your teen is normally angelic (and therefore, un-teenlike).

5) A sudden or a gradual change in friends. Clean to dirty. Preppy to grungy. Grungy to smelly. Et cetera.

Also know that there are different levels of trouble. It may be enough for him to meet with an in-school counselor. But you should also know that some teens are positively squeamish when it comes to seeking out a counselor or dealing with school personnel such as social workers or psychologists. (They're afraid to be seen entering the office.) And in-school help may not be enough help due to the counselors' or social workers' workload. Also, sometimes school is not in session for weeks and months on end, and your child may need therapy or counseling more often.

If your child is just not doing well enough socially, educationally, and emotionally, you may also wish to consider having your child undergo a complete psychological assessment. Part of this includes the use of standardized tests that usually cost money, which your health plan may not cover. Sometimes school districts will do some of the testing, upon request or because they think it is in order. In most communities, there are some mental health agencies that have sliding scales for patients of modest means. Some things to know:

1) If you do seek out professionals, there are three basic categories: social workers, psychologists, and psychiatrists. Social workers usually have a master's degree or bachelor's degree and are certified by a governmental or quasi-governmental entity. Psychologists gener-

ally work as counselors and researchers. Psychiatrists are medical doctors who can prescribe medication. If your child is on medication, he may also be referred to a psychopharmacologist, a medical doctor who may evaluate and monitor your teen's medication. Some agencies provide services of both psychologists and psychiatrists in the same facility, which is a plus. Your teen may then end up going to weekly therapy with a psychologist and have monthly visits with a psychiatrist who may check on the medication prescribed and also talk to your child.

2) If you don't know what health professional to go to, ask the school psychologist or social worker or guidance counselor where they'd recommend going. Your teen may feel uncomfortable going to a psychologist. Emphasize the fact that because it is confidential, no one will know. If your teen is very afraid of going to a local healthcare provider because he fears he will be seen by his peers or their parents, consider taking your teen to therapy in another town.

3) If your child was going to therapy and was on medication but refuses to go to therapy and take the medication, it is possible you will have to go to court to get

him the help he needs. If you do seek the help of the courts, you should find out what are the possible outcomes when going to court or the court's intake agency. You'll also want to know in advance if some other department or authority (such as a judge), and not you, will be the person or entity ultimately making decisions about your child. Find out whether by using the court system, your child could end up living someplace outside your home or in another county or state.

4) If you feel overwhelmed or your child just isn't doing well enough, enlist the aid of responsible extended family members if they exist. If you work long hours, you may need to acknowledge that you can't give your child the kind of supervision he needs. Is there a family friend or a member of your religious community who may be able to help? Sometimes the only thing standing between a child going into foster care or a facility is a caring adult the child and parent have a relationship with who offers assistance.

To Do: Trust Your Intuition

Do not dismiss the uneasy feelings you occasionally have but can't put your finger on. If you are speaking to your child on the phone when he is out or away for any length of time, or even if he isn't out for any length of time and he just doesn't sound like himself, or when he returns he does not look like himself, you must consider that something bad has happened and that he is afraid to tell you. Your job as a parent is to give your child the sense that you are safe enough and wise enough to help him when he gets in over his head—or is about to.

Even if your child isn't in trouble with the law or school, it doesn't mean he doesn't need help and guidance. But understand that you may not be equipped to help him in all his needs.

To Know

If he doesn't seem himself, that fact alone should raise the alarm. Teens have a high suicide rate and a considerable depression rate as well.

– Rule 35 –

Your teen will sometimes screw up in ways even a creative thinker wouldn't have thought of

Analyze the problem

The first thing to do is to characterize the nature of the screw-up. If your child has gotten into trouble with the law, he should have an attorney. If your teenager gets in trouble with the law or school or both, chances are quite good that he or she has a psychological problem. He may also possibly have a drug or alcohol dependency problem. You may not know your teen had this problem. Or maybe you know about the problem but have put your head in the sand. Without proper intervention, your child will likely find himself in the same or in a similar situation down the road, if not sooner.

To Know: Many Teens Don't Learn From Their Mistakes

This is because they lack maturity and experience in evaluating their conduct, or because they are operating below the radar screen and therefore continue unchecked for large blocks of time.

Part of the problem is, by the time some parents identify the problem, they have already lost control of the teen. Either the parents can't tell their kids what to do, or their kids have found ways to duck detection. Still others give up on their teens and effectively wash their hands of them. Your goal, then, is to not lose control, or if you have partially lost control, to gain it back rapidly. Think of yourself as a cowboy or cowgirl teaching a wild horse to submit to civilizing. It's that hard.

If Your Child Is Out of Control, You Need to Know

Some definitions of out-of-control (though not a comprehensive list):
1) Staying out all night or outrageously late
2) Using drugs
3) Binge drinking
4) Stealing
5) Destroying property
6) Beating people up, hitting, kicking, punching, spitting
7) Lying in major ways

What to Do If Your Teen Is Out of Control

Consider whether your child has a drug or alcohol abuse problem. You may want to start off a conversation by discussing the consequences, side effects, and legal ramifications of using drugs or alcohol. If you're not certain your child is actively using drugs, you may consider taking him for a consultation or assessment at a facility that assesses parties who may be in need of treatment. You may also want to explore whether your school district offers programs for students with drug problems or other problems that would require your child to attend an alternative program or school.

To Know: Teen Power Corrupts, and Absolute Teen Power Corrupts Absolutely (with Apologies to Lord Acton)

To regain control, reinstitute (or institute if you've never had) house rules. One thing you must require: that your teen attend school if he is below the age it is legally permissible to quit. And even then, you should emphasize the need to get a regular school degree. If he has dropped out of school, you must insist that he work at getting his General Equivalency Degree. If there are issues with drugs and alcohol (and even if there are not), your child should be required to let you know where he is at any given time and where he is staying. And, as always, be prepared to be lied to. Teens are inherently sneaky, and teens with drug or alcohol problems are even more so.

If you have decided to utilize the court system to get an order of protection or a restraining order against your child, prior to deciding a course of action, it would be wise to understand the legal ramifications of that order and the legal consequences of a violation of that order.

Conclusion

To be a parent of teenagers and survive requires good car insurance, a healthy ability to see strengths in one's children beyond the pile of grungy clothes that bedeck the room like mountains on the moon, and a belief that one's teens will, despite raging hormones and occasional evidence to the contrary, join society in a loose and meaningful sense of the word. To sum up: don't be lazy or sleep at the wheel of raising your teen; remember to spend quality time with your teens throughout their teendom; learn to say no; be a responsible adult; interact with other parents and the school; and if you're not a naturally suspicious type, immediately develop P.O.T.R. (Parent-of-Teenager Radar).

Successfully parenting teenagers requires a positive mental attitude, good values, common sense, a well-developed sense of responsibility toward one's own children and to society, a sense of humor, and cover-up cream to cover the dark circles under your eyes. Perhaps the last two items on that list count the most at the end of the day. Just remember: enjoy the journey together with your teen even though you may get a little carsick along the way (especially when you are teaching them to drive). Remember, a parent doesn't have to be war-weary. But know that some battle fatigue and grit and grime in one's boots are normal.

One Next-to-last General Rule About Teenagers That Needs No Further Explanation

Whenever you think something's not necessary with a teen, that's when it is.

One Final General Rule

Be an activist. Or, even better, try not to ever sleep during your teenager's teenage years.

Notes